GUIDE TO CERAMICS PAINTING

GUIDE TO CERAMICS PAINTING

NICOLETTA ZANARDI

Icon Editions

1817

HARPER & ROW, PUBLISHERS, New York

Cambridge, Philadelphia, San Francisco,
London, Mexico City, São Paulo, Sydney

Guide to Ceramics Painting
Translated by Mary Fitton
Copyright © 1982 Arnoldo Mondadori Editore S.p.A., Milan
English translation copyright © 1983
Arnoldo Mondadori Editore S.p.A., Milan

FIRST U.S. EDITION

LIBRARY OF CONGRESS
CATALOG CARD NUMBER: 83-48471
ISBN: 0-06-439000-4
ISBN: 0-06-430134-6 pbk.

CONTENTS

PAINTING ON CERAMICS

For the beginner this book is a progressive guide to the delightful art of china painting, from the earliest experimental steps to more ambitious projects; those who practise the art already may here, perhaps, learn more about such specialised techniques as the application of painted white relief, dabbed-on grounding and on-glaze gold, or the use of preserving-varnish.

The text is arranged in four parts. Part One, Tools and Techniques (page 15), lists the implements needed and explains their purpose. It then outlines the different methods of decorating pottery in colours or with gold, and describes the effects obtainable. Text and photographs show how pencil, pen and brush are held, how to sit correctly with the arm in the right position, how to handle the object being painted, and how to enlarge or reduce a design by means of a pantograph.

Part Two, Brushwork (page 53), analyses the painting process from the first brush-stroke to the rendering of flowers, landscapes, birds and animals, trees, fruit and vegetables, fish, shellfish, aquatic plants and oriental themes. This section also gives instructions for the brushing and dabbing-on of background colour; for decoration in white relief; for gilding, either on white or over colour; for executing borders and edging-lines; and for signing the piece before firing.

The forty or so patterns given in Part Three, Examples (page 157), require varying grades of skill and include vases, ornaments, tureens, lamp-bases, ashtrays, dinner-services and wall-plates. Designs are shown in outline drawing, with a colour photograph of each completed piece and step-by-step instructions in the text.

Part Four, Some Decorative Motifs (page 241), is a selection of motifs from many styles and periods—a fund of ideas to draw upon for your own designs.

Ceramics: majolica and porcelain

The word 'ceramic' can denote baked clay of many kinds. Majolica, sandstone, terracotta and porcelain are all ceramics of one sort or another.

Majolica is a porous, vitreous clay of Hispano-Moresque origin, the name possibly derived from Majorca, or from Malaga. It achieved rapid popularity in sixteenth-century Italy, and the Italian centres where it was made became famous throughout Europe; indeed, that at Faenza was so famous that majolica generally came to be known as faience ware.

Lending itself to rustic-style shapes and decoration, it is a more suitable material on which to learn china painting than the more costly

porcelain.

Porcelain is a hard, non-porous, translucent compound with a base of china-clay (kaolin) and feldspathic rock. It was first made in China and not until the beginning of the eighteenth century, at Meissen in Germany, was the secret of its composition discovered in the West; but once known it spread rapidly to every factory in Europe.

Porcelain objects are characterised by a purity of line which demands a more delicate style of ornamentation than majolica ware and, consequently, greater skill; so learn your craft on majolica.

The majolica and porcelain objects shown left and below respectively are readily distinguishable by their differing degrees of lustre.

Step by step: choosing a piece to decorate

There are at least four main stages in the process of china painting, beginning with the choice of a 'piece'—the object to be decorated. The vase illustrated below is of porcelain. Undecorated porcelain and majolica are sold by stockists who also supply brushes and other necessary equipment, and will advise on firing.

Painting on porcelain, however, is a final goal and not a starting-point, for it demands an exactitude in drawing and a sensibility in the use of colour which come only with perseverance. When you start on majolica there is no risk that minor imperfections or uncertainties of execution will spoil the simpler shapes and patterns: they may even add a certain unsophisticated charm.

Step by step: drawing the pattern

Having chosen something to decorate, your next step is to draw the design. In the illustration below, the bouquet, or flower pattern, has been drawn onto the vase with a pen.

Drawing can be learned, like anything else, but creative ability is not essential for ceramic work, since motifs can be traced and transferred to the surface by the method known as pouncing, or pricking-on. That is, the design is transferred as a series of black dots which are then joined up with pencil, pen or brush, depending on the type of decoration.

Beginners should gain experience with simple motif designs which can be very charming and effective.

Step by step: painting

After the outline has been carefully drawn over with a pen, the transferred pattern is next coloured. On the vase as seen here the pattern is partially painted, while part remains in outline.

Colour harmony is extremely important, no less so than the choice of design, which should be appropriate to both the medium—porcelain or majolica—and shape of the piece. Discordant colour, a disproportionate design, or a design that 'quarrels' with the shape, will inevitably ruin the result. Yet once the technical processes are mastered and a little know-how acquired, there is nothing intrinsically difficult about painting on china. Moreover, you will constantly pick up hints and develop expertise.

Step by step: firing

Below is the finished vase; the colours have now been fixed by firing and cannot be washed off. The firing of ceramics is done in the inner, fire-proof chamber of a special oven—the muffle-furnace, or kiln. The shop where you buy your pots and other supplies may well have a kiln, and also a banding-wheel with which circular ornamental lines can be marked.

Note that colours change in the heat of the kiln; pink, for instance, becomes appreciably lighter. It is only by practical knowledge of these tonal changes that you can assess what your work will look like on the finished article. The scheme suggested on page 38 may prove useful here.

TOOLS AND TECHNIQUES

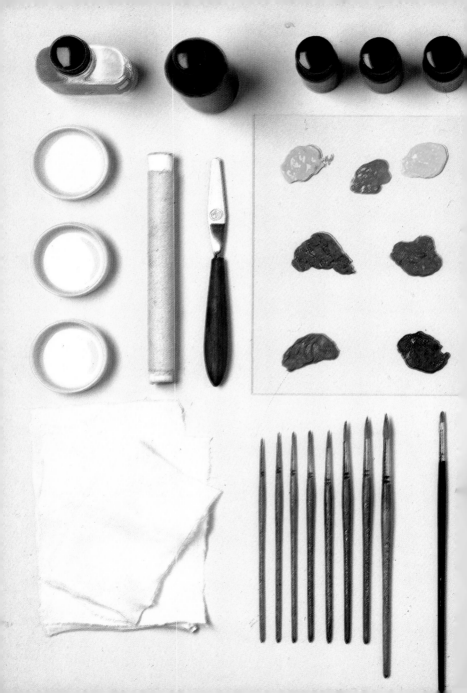

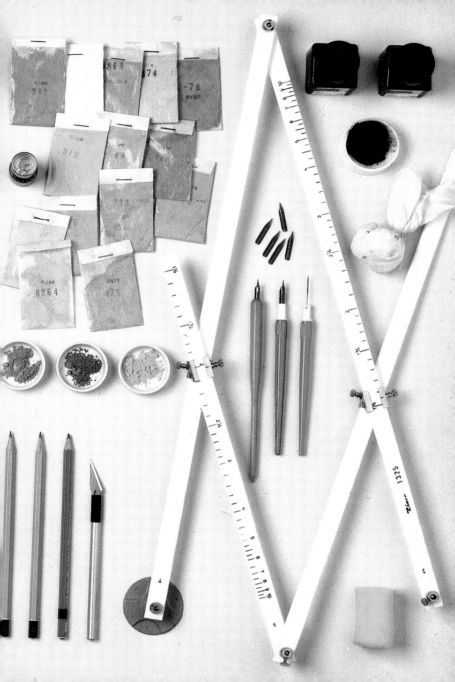

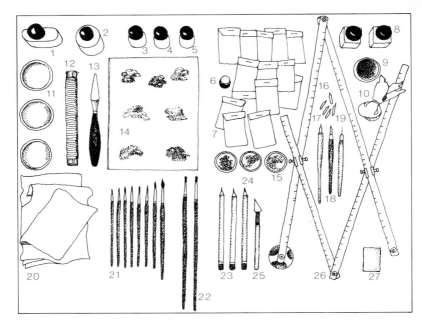

Illustrated on the two preceding pages are the implements and tools commonly employed in ceramic painting, and which will be most frequently mentioned in the text.

They are listed below and numbered on the key above, for easy identification.

 1 Oil of turpentine
 2 Preserving-varnish
 3 Oil of lavender
 4 Fat oil (*essence grasse*, or thick turpentine)
 5 Gold diluent
 6 Container for gold
 7 Packets of powdered pigment
 8 Containers for Chinese ink
 9 Pot of lampblack
10 Pad for applying lampblack when transferring designs
11 Containers for oils (small quantities)
12 Spun-glass burnisher for gold
13 Palette-knife
14 Glass palette
15 Pots of pigment
16 Nibs (various sizes)
17 Mapping pen (for use with Chinese ink)
18 Pen (for colouring)
19 Fine-pointed needle tool
20 Clean rags
21 Brushes
22 Brushes for ornamental lines, rims, etc
23 Drawing pencils
24 Soft pencil for use on ceramic surface
25 Scraper
26 Pantograph
27 Pad for dabbing-on background colour

TOOLS

Pencil

Drawing on ceramics is best done with a lithographic pencil, though an ordinary one will suffice, providing the lead is soft and smooth.

First, take the palette-knife and use it to blend some fat oil and turpentine; then prepare the surface of the ceramic, by rubbing it with a clean rag dipped in this mixture. Having allowed the piece to dry, prick the pattern on (see pages 31–3) and pencil over it. (This pencil line will disappear in the kiln.)

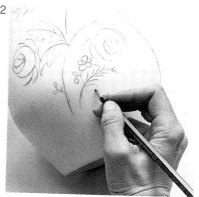

When drawing on the right half of a plate, hold the pencil in your right hand. Keep your right wrist on the work-table and grasp the plate firmly in the left hand (1).

For the left half of the drawing, the pencil is held in your right hand as before, but the wrist should now rest gently on the rim of the plate itself.

When painting a vase held in the left hand, it is usually easiest to rest not only the right wrist but part of the forearm, too, on the table (2).

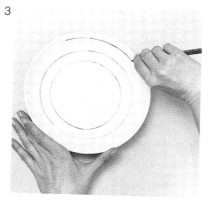

To draw a circular line on a plate, hold the pencil point between thumb, forefinger and third finger, and let it rest on the rim. The plate, in your left hand, is rotated slowly in an anti-clockwise direction, so that the pencil in your right hand automatically marks the required circle (3).

Pen

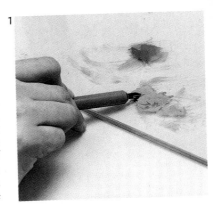

A very thin mapping pen is needed for marking designs onto tracing-paper with Chinese ink; one
should be kept for this purpose
only. You will also use a pen to
outline in colour the pattern you
have pricked onto the ceramic
surface (see page 33), and this is
certainly one of the trickiest of
the preliminary operations, since
the pen line, unlike that made in
pencil, remains clearly visible

3

after firing. The colours for it must therefore be mixed with the utmost care and the amount of fat oil must be absolutely right (see pages 24, 36). A fine line requires a tacky pigment, so increase the fat oil; for a darker line, use less.

To avoid damaging the nib, turn it face downwards and hold the pen horizontally as you dip it into the colour (1).

When inking a design onto a plate, the hand rests partly on the table and partly on the rim of the plate (2).

For a vase, the right elbow should stay on the table, while the hand rests lightly on the piece as you draw (3).

Palette-knife and palette

The palette-knife, for blending paint and oil and for removing any grains of undissolved pigment, is a stainless-steel blade some 9–10cm (about 4in) long, with a wooden handle. It can be bought at any shop supplying artists' materials and should be flexible and easy to manipulate, light but strong. It is a good idea to have more than one, so that it does not have to be cleaned each time a fresh colour is used.

The palette is essential for the preparation and mixing of colours as and when required and is cleaned, before and after use, with oil of turpentine and spirit. Instead of an artist's palette a glazed tile is used in china painting, or a small glass slab about 15×20cm (6×8in) in size. The glass, being smoother and non-absorbent, is preferable. Keep a separate palette for gold, and another for white relief.

33

33

The scraper

This indispensable instrument should never be out of reach. It is used to remove any surplus paint, splashes made as you work, or where you have painted over the outline or applied paint too thickly.

Use the scraper only when paint is dry and comes away readily; the point must always be sharp enough to lift the tiniest speck without scratching the surface (1).

You can also scrape clear large areas where paint has been applied, or background dabbed-on, too thickly (2). (In the latter case it might be quicker to wipe the area with a rag dipped in turpentine or spirit, but do this with great caution in order to avoid disaster.)

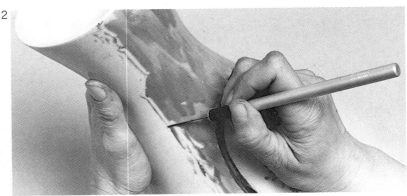

Pad for pricking-on

This is something to make rather than buy. Take some lampblack (obtainable from your stockist) with the palette-knife and place it in the middle of a square of clean cloth, preferably white (1). Gather the edges together, and tie them tightly with string or thread (2). This is your pad. As powdered lampblack is very fine and clinging, be sure to tie it securely at the top, so that none escapes.

The amount to use will differ with the size of pattern you are dealing with, but roughly speaking a pad should be no larger than 4–5cm (1½–2in) in diameter. If no lampblack is available you can substitute pencil-leads broken up and powdered.

With this pad, as explained on page 32, a design, perforated on

tracing-paper, is transferred onto the piece you are painting. The lampblack, dabbed onto the tracing-paper, will penetrate the perforations and reproduce the pattern on the surface beneath. This technique has been used since earliest times and enables the least adroit of draughtsmen to decorate pottery.

Oils

Oil is the medium with which pigments are mixed. Four oils are used in ceramic painting and each has its particular properties.

Oil of turpentine A solvent for mixing powdered colours and for dissolving any which have become hardened by exposure to the air, or have become too thick; also for cleaning brushes and palette.

Oil of lavender Used, with turpentine and fat oil, in preparing colour for a dabbed-on ground (see page 42); also, in smaller quantities, for brush-painted background colours (see page 41) and for the dark blue in some oriental patterns (pages 138–9).

Gold diluent Liquid gold may condense on keeping, and is thinned down with minimal quantities of diluent. This oil is also

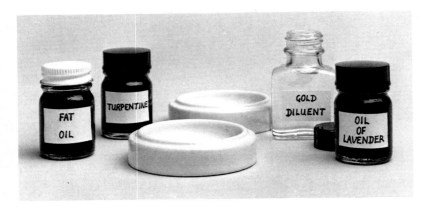

Fat oil Essential for bringing pigments to their required consistency after mixture with turpentine (see page 36). The amount of fat oil determines the degree of fluidity of the paint—in other words, how tacky the paint will be. Too much fat oil, and the paint will not dry; too little, and it dries as you put it on. You may attempt to remedy matters with more pigment or more oil respectively, but it is usually better to start again.

necessary for pen-writing in gold (see page 45).

Containers for turpentine

Turpentine is often sold in inconveniently large bottles or tins. As it is constantly needed, keep small amounts handy in little glass or metal containers, into which you can dip your palette-knife. It is highly inflammable and must not be stored near heat.

Brushes

These should be carefully chosen, in the sizes suitable for the work envisaged and with bristles of superior quality. Stockists have a vast selection, but sable-hair brushes are invariably softer and more flexible; they 'carry' the paint better. Try to have more than one of each size, as you can then change colours without delay and are less likely to find yourself suddenly lost for a brush in the middle of a design.

Brushes are numbered according to thickness—low numbers for thin tips, high numbers for thicker ones. (The thicker the tip, the darker the stroke will be.) Illustrated below are those you should begin with.

One or two of sizes 0, 1 and 6 should be sufficient, but buy two, or even four, of sizes 2, 3, 4 and 5. Treat the tips with respect,

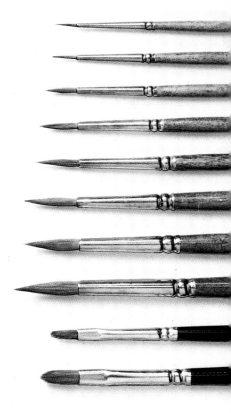

No 0 For outlining small flowers and thin stems

No 1 For painting small flowers (cornflowers, etc)

No 2 For shading small flowers (marguerites, etc); for white relief and gold

No 3 For painting flowers such as roses and chrysanthemums; small stems and leaves; handles

No 4 For painting flowers such as peonies and poppies; leaves; trees; houses; and geometrical motifs

No 5 For painting leaves and flowers of large bouquets; for fish; vegetables; birds; to apply preserving-varnish

No 6 For large landscape areas, eg fields and terraces; for backgrounds— rocks, sky, water, etc

No 7 For borders or broad ornamental lines and dabbed-on grounding

Flat brush For borders or ornamental lines on tea-cups, ashtrays, pintrays

Flat brush For borders painted with a loaded brush, on vases, plates, jugs

25

as they are useless after contact with other pigments.

To take up paint from your palette, put the tip of the brush into the pigment and lift no more than will adhere to it (1). To prevent the formation of globules on the brush, roll the tip in the paint with a rapid semicircular movement, so that the bristles flatten out (2) and the surplus is expelled.

To clean the brush for a fresh colour, dip it into turpentine, shake it slightly to dislodge the paint and wipe it on a clean rag on the work-table (3).

The brush is held in exactly the same way as are the pen and pencil for decorating a vase (4) or a plate (5). Do not allow globules of paint to form.

whether when painting or cleaning them, to ensure they are not damaged. A brush should be dipped in turpentine and dried on a clean rag every time a fresh pure colour is taken up, though you may of course omit this precaution if several colours are mixed on the palette. Always clean your brush in turpentine when you finish work, or paint will dry on the tip.

No 2 brushes, for gold and for white relief, are kept separately,

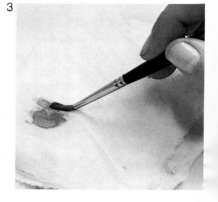

TECHNIQUES

Subdivision of a circle

Occasionally a piece has to be divided into equal sections for decoration and if it is a circular object, such as a lid or plate, these divisions are calculated on paper.

First, with a pair of compasses, describe a circle of the same size as the piece itself, and mark the diameter A – C –B. With the com-

passes at A and a radius of more than half the diameter, describe an arc above point C; then another, with the same radius, from point B. These two arcs will intersect at D. The perpendicular C–D will pass through the circumference at E and may be extended to give the diameter E–F. With two diameters, the circle is divided into four equal parts. Similarly, point G is found by describing arcs based on E and A; then point G1, with arcs based on E and B

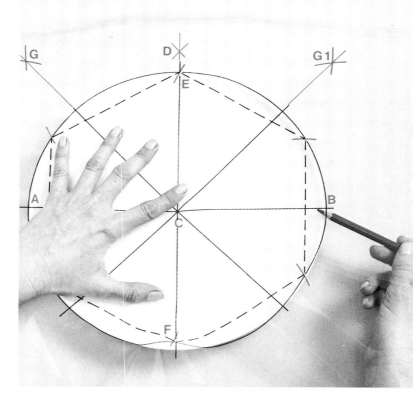

Lines C–G and C–G1 may then be produced to divide the circle into eight. For division into six parts, arcs with radius E–C and F–C are described from points E and F, intersecting the circumference to give four more points which, linked with E and F as shown by the dotted lines in the diagram opposite, will form a hexagon.

This is the most reliable method for the accurate subdivision of a plate.

Subdivision of a vase

By the same process a vase may be marked off into regular sections. Your paper circle will match the mouth of the vase (or its base if the top is not circular), across which it is placed. Points A to F are then found on the rim. With the aid of a plumb-line establish the perpendicular and mark it in pencil. By moving the plumb-line from point to point on the rim you may divide the whole piece.

The pantograph

This is a device, obtainable from office stationers, with which a design is copied onto a piece of paper on a greater (1) or smaller (2) scale than the original. For instance, it could be used to enlarge designs that have had to be scaled down to fit the pages of this book.

The four parallel bars are marked in millimetres and are screwed together. One end is fixed to the table and the chosen pattern traced by one metal point while another repeats it in pencil on tracing-paper. The instrument can be adjusted by means of small numbered notches to varying angles and degrees of enlargement, making it possible to adapt the same pattern to several sizes, as, for example, when it is required for a complete dinner-service.

Transferring a design by the-pricking-on process

The first step in the transfer of a design to a ceramic surface is to put it onto tracing-paper. When taking it from a book, or from a single sheet, all you do is hold or tape the tracing-paper firmly in place and trace the pattern in Chinese ink with a mapping pen (1).

Next, put this paper, inked side downwards, onto a layer of thick cloth—flannel or some similar material—and with a fine point prick over the whole design, making sure that nothing is omitted (2).

The procedure for copying from a solid object, though naturally less straightforward, is identical and with a little patience yields the same satisfactory result.

Should you wish to take several copies at once, pin extra

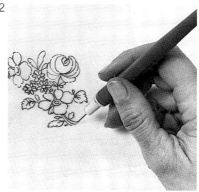

2

sheets of tracing-paper below that on which you have inked the design; the perforations in the top sheet will go through to the others (see Fig 4, page 32). It is thus quite simple to build up a valuable collection of designs which may prove useful, particularly when an original becomes tattered with use.

4

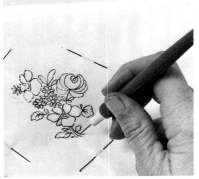

5

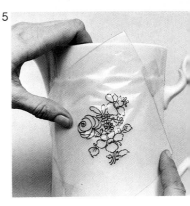

Tape the sheet with the perforated design to the ceramic you are going to paint (5), and remember that its placing at this stage is all-important; much of the final effect depends on how well the design enhances the function and shape of the piece, so some thought should be given to this before you begin.

6

Next comes the actual 'pricking-on', or pouncing. The pad described on page 23 is pressed gently onto the perforated paper, so that the lampblack penetrates every tiny hole of the design (6). When the tracing-paper is removed, the dotted design will remain on the surface of the pot (8). Finally, for a clearer and continuous line, join up the dots with pen or pencil (9). If done in pen, this outline will be visible after firing and the colour chosen should therefore suit the type of design. An outline colour, in accordance with the established traditions of ceramic decoration, is suggested for each design given in this book,

7

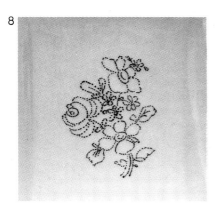

but those who prefer to use ideas from other sources will be guided by experience and individual taste.

Holding a plate

When painting round the rim of a plate, hold it on the flat of your left hand and tilted slightly towards you. The back of your hand, and possibly part of your left forearm, rests on the work-table, so that the lower edge of the plate is supported on the table (see below). This is the best and least tiring position for the beginner, and the easiest way to paint is to start at the bottom, in the middle. Alternatively, you may hold the plate on your palm horizontally and turn it, slowly and gradually, as you work; but this will certainly be less secure, for the edge has nothing to rest on, and you must therefore keep your left forearm on the table. The little finger of the right hand may just touch the edge of the plate, to guard against shaking and vibration.

Holding a vase

A vase is usually held in the left hand, slightly tilted, with its base on the table. As vases tend to be large and heavy objects, it is as well to rest part of the left forearm on the table; while, to ensure a steady hand, the right arm should also be firmly supported on the table. When painting the upper edge of the base, however, raise the right forearm and lean on the elbow alone, so that your brush-hand is at the correct height.

Alternatively, you can put the vase on its side on the table and grip it in the left hand as you paint with the right. Your elbow then rests on the table and the brush is perpendicular to the work.

Paint

Special paints for what is known as the 'soft firing' of ceramics— the *petit feu*, at temperatures between 650° −815°C (1,200°− 1,500°F)—are sold, generally in 10g packets, by suppliers of artists' materials.

Remove the pigment from the packet with a palette-knife, and place it on the palette (1). Then thoroughly mix it with oil of turpentine until it is neither too

On the other hand, slow-drying paint which remains wet once painted on the ceramic is too oily; it will mar everything by rising above the glaze when fired, and scaling off. The way colours are mixed is thus another determining factor in the success or failure of a project.

The basic colours, which should always be to hand, are:

Pink This is a rather difficult colour, in that it can be hard to

liquid nor too thick (2). Lastly, add a drop or two of fat oil (3) and thoroughly mix again (4) whereupon the paint will be fluid enough to spread with a brush on the ceramic. The correct proportions are approximatey 40 per cent pigment, 40 per cent turpentine and 20 per cent fat oil.

The quality of the colours obtained depends on the correct consistency of the paint. If paint dries immediately, it lacks body and more fat oil must be added.

spread, whether in painting a design or dabbing-on a background. An extra drop of fat oil or, better, two or three drops of lavender oil, may help. It should be very well mixed.

Rose-purple Another difficult colour, often used for the pen outline of flowers, especially in patterns of oriental type.

Red This can mean anything from glowing tomato to red-

2

brown terracotta, but all shades spread easily. Red loses much of its tone in firing if in contact with any other colour, so beware of mixtures and certainly avoid yellow, in conjunction with which it can disappear entirely. On majolica it may alter and darken in firing, but it will retain its brightness on porcelain which is less absorbent.

Black Spreads well; often used for pen outlines.

3

4

Yellow The various shades of yellow are all easy to apply, needing little fat oil.

Brown The lighter browns, from the yellow to tobacco tones, will spread easily and do not require much fat oil; the darker shades are harder to work.

Blue The lighter, sky-blue and lavender, shades spread well whereas the darker ones require more fat oil.

37

The test palette

Do not rush to buy every colour in the shop when you begin ceramic painting; you will have enough with those already mentioned. The main thing is to save yourself from unpleasant surprise and disappointment by discovering all you can about the preparation and application of colours, and what happens to them in the kiln.

A quick and practical way of doing this is to take a glazed white tile, or a porcelain plate, pencil it approximately into squares, and paint each square a different colour. Give some squares one coat, others two or three layers of paint, so that the colours are seen in increasing thickness; allow each layer to dry before applying the next and make all your brushstrokes in the same direction. When fired, the tile will reveal the characteristics of any given colour, showing you how much pigment, turpentine and fat oil to use, what shades result from added layers of paint, and how it reacts to the kiln. The illustration opposite demonstrates an experimental test tile on which a range of tones has been achieved. (Top to bottom: rose-purple, geranium red, yellow, blue, green and brown.)

Keep a note of what you do—what colour and how many layers were applied to which squares, what tones a colour assumed at various kiln temperatures, and anything else that may be useful

to know in the future. A good plan is to copy the tile or plate on paper and to annotate the squares; with this paper and the fired tile you have a record available for constant consultation. For a simpler and even quicker method number the squares on the tile.

With this as a base you can build up the palette which indicates your needs and tastes; it will be a personal preference, for the choice, save when dictated by external considerations, is entirely yours. Thus, some may favour the whole gamut of yellows and not much else, others incline to the blues, the reds and so on. A more or less complete range for ceramic work would include about forty shades, though most people get along with fewer. The good china-painter is not proclaimed by a dazzling rainbow of tints, but rather by the clean line of a design, its aptness and harmony, by an eye for colour combination, and patience. With patience you will repeat your early attempts until skill and confidence are gained; in particular you will be rewarded for the time spent in assembling a test palette, which you will find increasingly helpful as you progress.

A tip to speed up the drying of colours: use the kitchen stove. Heat the oven, turn it off and put the painted pot inside for a moment or two. This ensures that a piece is properly dry between each stage of the work, and when you take it for firing.

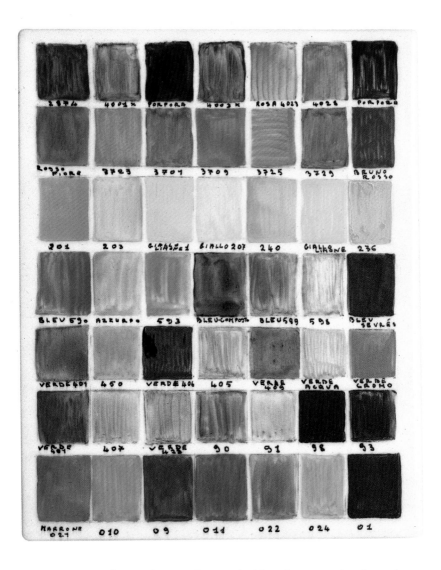

An experimental test tile provides a valuable reference point for colour tones and characteristics.

Preserving-varnish

When dabbing-on a background (see page 42) you may wish to isolate some of the surface from the background colouring. For this purpose varnish is used, in a careful, step-by-step process.

First prick the design onto the piece, outline it in pen, and paint it.

Next, draw a border round the design with a No 3 or 4 brush dipped in varnish. When deciding how wide to make this border, bear in mind that it is to remain white (see below). Once the design is isolated you may dab-on the background around the varnish border.

When the background is finished, remove the varnish with a scraper; or, if a clean rag is pressed firmly on it and then removed, the varnish will come away quite easily.

Brushed-on monotone grounding

We speak of a 'brushed-on' grounding when the entire white ground of a piece, except the area taken up by the decoration, is brush-painted in a single, flat colour. One result of this is that the design, already drawn and painted, will be emphasised and will stand out strongly.

The pigment should be well dissolved in turpentine. Then a very little fat oil is added—less than when mixing paint for a design (see page 36)—together with two or three drops of oil of lavender.

Paint for grounding must be kept moist, so stir it now and again with the palette-knife and add a few drops of turpentine or lavender oil if necessary. For small areas, and for areas adjacent to the pattern (see Figs 1 and 2,

page 41), use a No 2 brush; for larger areas, a No 3 (see vase on page 237).

For a compact and uniform effect the brush-strokes should be short, close together and all in the same downward direction.

Dabbed-on grounding

The whole, or a large and well defined area, of the surface may also be 'dabbed-on' in one colour by means of a foam rubber pad (not to be confused with the pad employed for pricking-on, described on page 23) about 3–4cm (1–1½in) in diameter.

Prepare all the paint you require in a single batch and do not stop once you begin; you could never get just the same shade again, nor could you continue when the part already done was dry. Mix the paint (1) in approximately the following proportions: 3 parts of pigment, 1 part of turpentine, 1 part of lavender oil and 1 part of fat oil. Here again, repeated experiment is the surest guide. To ascertain whether the quantities are right, make two or three brush-strokes on the surface you are decorating and dab them quickly with the foam rubber pad. If the paint is too tacky, add oil of lavender or

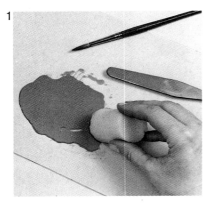

more powdered pigment; if it dries immediately, more fat oil is needed. But if it spreads evenly the consistency is correct; wipe out the trial strokes with a clean rag dipped in spirit or turpentine and begin.

The pad may be dipped in colour and dabbed straight onto the surface, or alternatively the whole surface can first be painted with a brush. Direct dabbing is suitable for small objects and areas, but for larger pieces, where

wide, close, downward strokes proceeding from left to right, and when the area is covered start the dabbing-on without delay. This will blend the paint and conceal any imperfections in the brush-work. Leave the piece to dry for twenty-four hours before firing.

all or most of the surface is to be covered, preliminary painting is advised. Do not forget to protect those sections already decorated by a border of preserving-varnish.

Dab the piece lightly and regularly with the pad, letting the paint overlap so that it may be evenly distributed (2).

If you brush-paint first, do so as fast as you can, for the colour must not dry while you are dabbing-on. Use a No 7 brush and

Painted white relief

As its name implies, white relief is a decoration contrived with thicker-than-normal white paint. The white pigment is well mixed with turpentine and a little fat oil to a chalky consistency, and a small amount taken up on a No 2 brush. Without 'pulling' it, make small close-set dots on the surface, about one millimetre thick.

The two things to watch are the thickness of the dots, which should stand out enough to give a relief effect; and the proper mixing of the paint. Any mistake with one or the other, and the dots may break off when fired.

If this white relief is to be combined with colours, it should be done when the coloured part of the design is finished to ensure a perfect white.

Gold

Gold is bought in small sealed tubes and should be shaken vigorously before use, as the grains may have settled and need to be mixed up again. Close the tube securely afterwards, or the gold will evaporate and be wasted; keep it away from heat.

Transfer gold from the tube to your palette with a glass rod or palette-knife. Use diluent only if it has thickened in the tube, and then in minute quantities, for the gilding will assume a dark, reddish tone on firing if too much is added.

Take the gold from the palette onto a pen or brush: the pen for lettering and outlines, the brush for gilded patterns. The black appearance it assumes on coming into contact with the surface is

1

45

temporary, and its true colour will emerge after it has been fixed in the kiln.

To write an initial, hold the pen as shown in Fig 1 on page 45. Press a little harder to widen the stroke with the curve of the letter, and very lightly along the outside of the letter, where the line must be continuous and distinct.

For outlining a pattern you need as steady a hand as possible; try resting your right palm or little finger on the edge of the plate or vase—just enough to give some support—as you rotate the piece slowly with the left hand (see Fig 2, page 45).

For ornamental motifs (3) use a No 2 brush and put on the gold in compact, even strokes; it should not be too thick. Any scraping off of errors must be done when it is perfectly dry, otherwise dark, indelible smudges will remain.

When you finish, scrupulously clean the brush or pen-nib with gold diluent.

3

Borders

Borders, whether of geometrical motifs or bands of uniform colour, occur more often on majolica ware than porcelain.

They are executed with a flat brush, or with a No 4 or No 7, in a range of fairly strong colours—dark blue, terracotta, green or chestnut-brown—which are mixed without too much fat oil and kept fluid by the addition of a

1

few drops of oil of lavender, and of turpentine at the first sign of congealing.

A geometrical border is usually enclosed in narrow parallel lines of the same colour; and although an obviously 'hand-made' and occasionally 'wavy edging has its charm, it is best to draw these lines on a banding-wheel at your local kiln.

Geometrical patterns are pricked-on, as previously explained, and outlined in pencil. They are then painted with short, downward strokes, which should be close together in order to achieve a uniform effect (1). Should any unwanted shading creep in it can be rectified with another, lighter brushing when the first is absolutely dry.

If your border is a ribbon of solid colour (2)—which is simpler and quicker to do—it is also helpful to mark the double outline in pencil first. Proceed as for a geometrical design.

Ornamental lines

Whereas borders are themselves a decoration, ornamental lines and edgings are the finishing touches when the main decorative scheme is already complete. You must not overdo them, however, no matter how pretty and often highly effective they may be; too many can produce an unwelcome impression of cluttering the design.

Whether in the form of plain lines along the sides or rim of a piece, or as a repeating pattern of small fanciful motifs, they should accord with the shape and purpose of the object, and are always carried out in one colour or in gold.

Accuracy is absolutely essential for the plain line which should therefore be drawn on a banding-wheel. More complicated motifs are drawn free-hand. Paint with a flat brush, or with a No 3 or 7. See that the pigment

stays fluid as you work, and that the colour chosen complements the rest of the design.

The little 'dog's-tooth' pattern is an attractive edging, and presents no difficulty. Begin by making parallel lines in pencil, as explained on page 19. These lines are usually 3–4mm apart, but the distance may be altered in proportion to the size and shape of the piece. Between them draw tiny semicircles, also in pencil, with the curves facing inwards. These are then filled in with brush-painted colour (1).

It is advisable to describe an ornamental line round the rim or neck of a vase on a banding-wheel, especially on porcelain, although if the piece has a rustic-style decoration you could draw it yourself: hold the brush horizontally at right angles to the surface and slowly rotate the vase in your left hand (2).

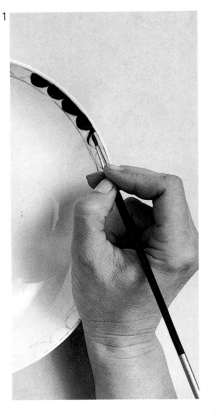

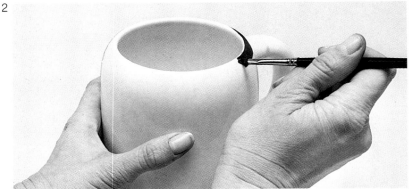

Handles

Many ceramics—for example, teapots, cups, tall amphora-type jars, some plates—have one or two handles. These may be left plain white, but the customary decoration in gilding or colour shows a regard for detail which lends distinction to the whole piece.

Needless to say, there is no room for decorative patterns as such, but for line-ornament only. This frequently narrows from top to bottom and may have arabesques to left and right. Only occasionally are small stylised leaves or flowerets added as a repeat of the main design.

Use the dominant colour of the main design, or match it if in monochrome. With a No 3 brush paint down the length of the handle, starting from the top, where the stroke will be heaviest to produce a broad line. Gradually diminish the pressure of the stroke towards the bottom, and be sure that a good layer of paint is applied (1).

For gilding the method is the same (2). Although gold spreads more readily and is therefore easier to work with, it must not, as noted on page 46, be applied too thickly in case it cracks on firing and impairs the decoration. Use a loaded brush and flat, even strokes.

Hinges

The lids of small ceramic objects are often secured by metal hinges, generally gilded. These are sold by suppliers of undecorated china and are obtainable in a range of mountings to fit various jars, boxes, ashtrays and so on, such as those illustrated.

The small lidded boxes, of different shapes and sizes are typical, and were particularly popular in eighteenth-century France (see pages 184–5): collectable items, despite their diverse uses.

There is the right kind of hinge for every object. It is added after firing and is therefore bought separately, as is the special glue. (Your supplier will stock this as well. Always read the instructions, which vary from one brand to another.)

A hinged lid will enhance the appearance and aesthetic appeal

of the object but only when perfectly placed in relation to the
piece's form and decoration. If
the lid itself is decorated, paint
and fire it before the hinge is
attached.

51

Cleaning and signing

When the painting is complete, all you have to do is clean the piece meticulously, sign it and take it to the kiln.

Cleaning involves the removal of any marks or smudges of pigment so that the outlines are clear and sharp. Use a clean white rag dipped in turpentine or spirit; spirit is better, as turpentine can leave the surface slightly greasy. Thick bits of dried paint are removed with the scraper.

Sign your work with a pen—either with your initials or your full name as you choose, perhaps adding 'Painted by hand', or *Peint à la main*, if you prefer. This is the finishing touch before taking the piece to be fired when the lustre of the colours will be brought out by the heat of the kiln.

A final caution: never be tempted to paint any old pottery you happen to have in the house. Its reaction to firing is unpredictable and may be disastrous.

BRUSHWORK

FIRST STROKES WITH BRUSH AND PEN: FLOWERS

Small flowers

Since flowers are so often the theme of china decoration, let your first experiment be the painting of a flower. Take an ordinary plate or something similar with a white surface, which is easy to handle and paint, and mix your colours according to the instructions on page 36. You will need pink or yellow, and green for the calyx and stalk. With a No 3 brush transfer a drop of colour to the plate (1a). Now press the brush down slightly on this drop, so that the bristles spread out, and 'pull' the paint towards you, making a left-hand curve. Curve another stroke to the right, and you have painted a petal with a small white space in the middle (1b). If this space is left white, or filled in with a paler shade when the side-strokes are dry, the flower will appear to be more luminous.

Next add two more petals, one on each side, and link the three with a short left-to-right stroke, like a shell, for the calyx. An oblique downwards stroke with the point of the brush for the stem (1c), and your first flower is done.

As a second step you might paint a stylised cornflower (2)

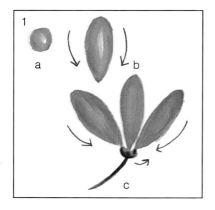

with blue for the petals, yellow for the disc, green for leaves and stem and red for the stamens. Arrows in the illustration show the direction in which to work. Each petal is formed by placing a few dots of colour at the outermost point of the petals and pulling the paint towards you.

For the marguerite (3) begin by painting the yellow disc, then with a pencil mark a circle as a guideline for painting the petals; the upper petals should be bright-er and deeper in tone than the lower. Other flowers to try are those illustrated in Fig 4a and the tiny, very ornamental blue ones (4b). The red corolla of the for-mer is brushed in with a single stroke, and a ring of white is left visible between corolla and yel-low disc (4a).

Each petal of the little blue flower is darker at the edges than the centre; leaves and stems are painted in green with a No 1 brush.

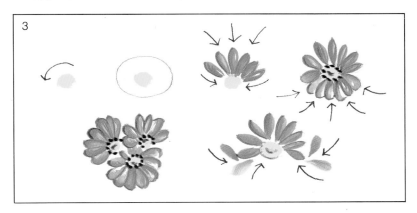

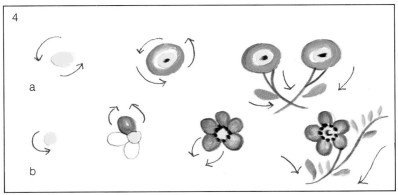

First compositions

Having mastered the technique of painting single flowers, you can begin to arrange them in small compositions of your own. Choose a No 2 or 3 brush for petals and leaves and a No 1 for stems and outlines.

To paint a posy, or small bouquet, draw it first in outline with pencil or brush. This outline, if brushed, should match the monochrome for a monochrome

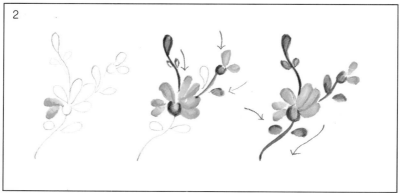

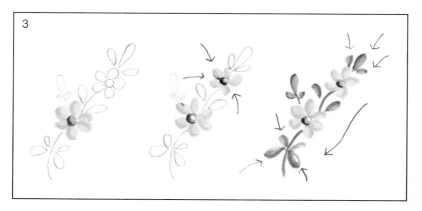

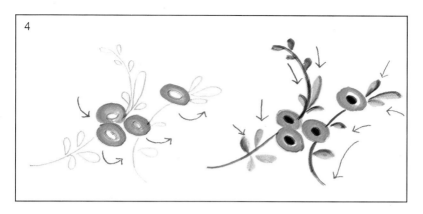

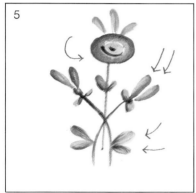

design; where several colours are planned, use black or chestnut-brown, without too much fat oil in the mixture, as a vigorous contour is desirable, whereas for the actual painting the colour should be more fluid.

Illustrations 2, 3, 4 and 6 show simple bouquet designs in their various stages—the preliminary sketch, the order in which they should be painted and the end result. Arrows indicate the direction of the brush-strokes.

More flowers: pricking-on and pen-drawing

The method, explained on page 31, of pricking-on a design and going over it in colour with a pen is also employed for flowers, foliage, small figures and landscapes, especially those in the oriental style.

Considerable skill is called for in joining up the dots of lamp-black on the surface with a pen, thus redrawing the pattern with a continuous outline. Proficiency in the whole delicate business of transferring a design from tracing-paper to ceramic is gained only through practice.

When the pen line is dry you may start brush-painting. This takes more time and is more complicated than brush-drawing, for now you must keep within the outline and work with greater precision.

The outlines of the bouquets shown in Fig 1 are pen-drawn, with the petals and leaves painted as described in the previous pages.

Place several small dots close together, on the ceramic surface and blend them with the brush. The stroke is always shaded from dark to light, and may even fade into the white background.

To shade a petal, move the brush in a sweeping, almost spiral, stroke from left to right, at the same time moving from the tip towards the base (2a).

The same stroke, taken in the direction indicated by the arrows,

1

is used for the petals of the oriental-type flower in Fig 2b.

For the flowers in Fig 2c, again follow the arrows with a similar brush-stroke, working towards the centre.

The marguerite (2d) is shown in two stages; first pen-drawn and partially painted, and then the finished flower.

Roses

By now you should be ready to tackle the queen of flowers. So often is it the focal point of a bouquet, so obviously the leading floral motif in china decoration, that it is worth learning to render its beauty and colour as well as possible.

Figs 1 and 2 show how the shape of a rose is built up and painted, with arrows, as before, to guide your brush-strokes. Begin by sketching the basic schematic structure of the flower in pen or pencil (1). If in pen, use a fairly dark tint—rose-purple, for instance, to outline a pink flower.

Next, prepare the colours: pale or dark pink, purple or yellow, which should certainly be more fluid than usual, for there is a lot of shading to do. For fluidity, and consequent facility of shading, lavender oil is added to the fat oil when mixing (see page 36). The best brush to use is a No 3 or 4.

You should, of course, aim to judge the effect of every stroke as you go along, but to retouch, wait until the surface is dry.

The central part of the rose is darker than the surrounding petals, and shaded in soft, downward strokes (2a). For the bulk of the flower, make your strokes small and short, and suggest its roundness by slight shading, downwards on the left side, upwards on the right, in an almost circular movement (2b). The petals above eye-level should have less colour than those below, and they should all curve in harmony with the overall shape of the flower (2c).

As for the centre of the rose, the brush-strokes for the petals should be light and quick, shading off to the very palest tone to give a luminous effect.

By following these instructions you will build up a complete rose (2d), and through careful practice and trial and error your roses will improve all the time giving an increasing sense of satisfaction.

2

a

b

c

d

More roses: closed and open buds

Since, as already pointed out, the rose is the prime subject for ceramic decoration, it is as well to be able to paint its different aspects—both in bud and half opened as well as experimental shapes—and incorporate these into more complex designs.

For an unopened bud (1), use a No 4 brush and start with the central petal, painting in the direction of the arrow (1a). Add a pair of sepals to right and left of it, joined at the base. The usual downward brush-stroke is employed (see page 54), and for this you must hold the piece upside down (1b, 1c). Then, still with the piece reversed, paint a second pair of outer sepals, each resembling a comma (1d, 1e). The calyx from which the bud is growing is a horizontal concave line (1f). For

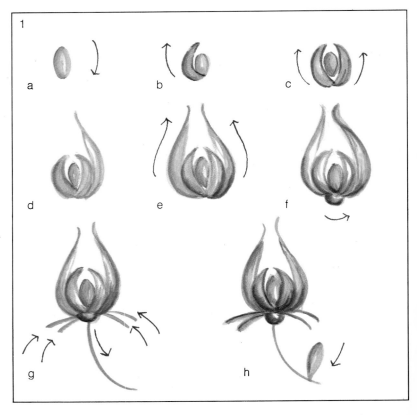

the 'whiskers' at the base of the bud, two on each side, move your brush upwards and inwards (1g). The stem is a green curve painted downwards from the calyx (1g) and the stroke for the tiny leaf is taken towards, not from, the stem (1h).

The first petal of a half-opened rose (2) is painted from its left-hand edge with vertical outward strokes (2a); the second is painted from the centre of the flower towards the right-hand edge (2b). Linking these two is a third petal, shaded from top to bottom as the work is held upside down (2c). Use circular strokes for the heart of the rose, which is darkest in the middle, and shade them to convey roundness (2d). The arrows (2e, 2f, 2g, 2h) show how subsequent petals are added and the last petal at the base of the rose consists of two equal, inward-moving strokes (2i).

Violet, cornflower, daffodil, lily

These are among the classic flowers of ceramic decoration, and are used either as single motifs or combined with other elements in composite designs.

Begin by drawing the outline of your chosen flower in pen, in its natural colour, or in black. The violets in Fig 1 show how this outline is progressively filled in — using violet with a No 3 or 4 brush. Paint outwards from the middle of the flower, following the shape of the petal and shading the colour off so that it is palest at the tip.

The cornflower (2) is shown at three successive stages. Here, too, the petals are shaded outwards from the base. The effect of light and shade on stem, leaves and calyx is suggested with lighter and heavier strokes respectively. Use a No 2 brush.

The daffodil (3) is shaded, like

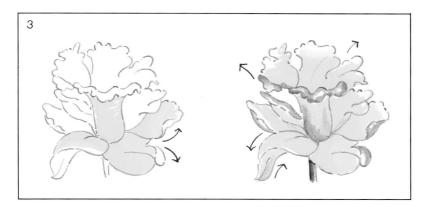

the others, outwards from the centre, so that the colour is darkest at the heart of the flower, growing lighter at the edges. Naturally the basic tint is yellow in varying tones: pale for the petals in full light, dark on the central trumpet and for the parts in shadow. Use a No 4 brush.

The pink lily (4) is shown at two successive stages of painting. Once more, work from the centre to the outer edges, this time with a No 2 brush, shading off con-

tinually in light, curving strokes. Allow the pink colour to dry before making the rose-purple spots on the petals. The pistils are drawn in lightly, in black, with a pen.

Tulips

For these two examples, the technique, illustrated step by step, is again that of brush-painting over a preliminary ´pen- or pencil-drawing. Try experimenting with the different aspects of tulips to incorporate in your own designs.

Colours for the first tulip are pale yellow, red, green and black; the brush is a No 2 or 3. Start with a pen outline in red (1a), then, with yellow, brush-paint almost half of the petals from the tips downwards. Changing to red, bring the colour up from the base to meet the yellow (1b, 1c). Where the two colours meet the greatest care must be taken, since red will fade, or even disappear completely, in the firing if placed on top of yellow. The stem is painted in light and dark green when the flower is complete and the paint dry; add the black pistils with a pen (1d).

For the violet-coloured tulip

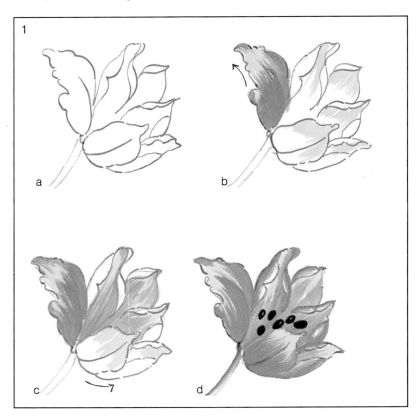

(2) the preliminary drawing is in pencil but the same brush, a No 2 or 3, is used for the painting. Colour the petals one by one, first the right and then the left-hand section, in slightly curving, lengthwise strokes, starting at the tip (2b, 2c).

To give the feeling of depth, the colour of the petals varies in density; the side petals and the central one in the foreground are shaded more darkly than those further back (2d, 2e).

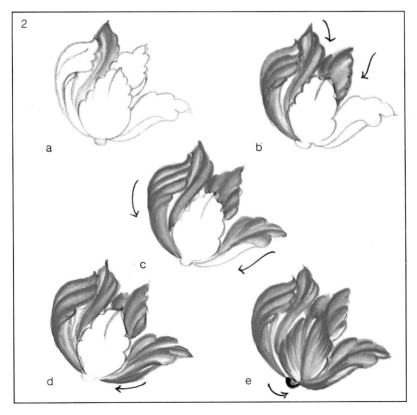

2

a

b

c

d

e

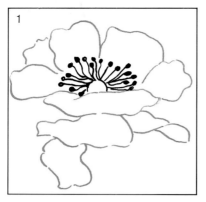

Poppies

The wild poppy is of great decorative value, and the design in Fig 2 is a charming arrangement of two open flowers, leaves, stems and buds.

Trace the design, prick it onto the surface and pen-draw the outline. For the painting use a No 4 brush.

The pen outline of the stem and leaves is chestnut-brown, that of the flowers and buds, terracotta. The most prominent flower is shown in outline in Fig 1, though the stamens are not in fact drawn in until after it is painted.

Pay close attention to the recommended brush-strokes used in building up the petals, since the volume and fullness of the flower should be suggested by gradations of colour. The paint must always be pulled towards you and the piece therefore turned slowly, so that you are always working in the right direction.

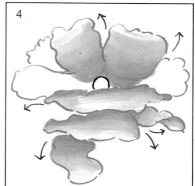

Study the directional arrows in Figs 3, 4 and 6.

The petals pointing towards the stem are painted from the centre outwards as shown in Fig 3.

The middle petals of the large flower are shaded by slightly curved strokes, beginning from the centre and becoming progressively lighter as they approach the tip (4).

The smallest leaves may be pale green; others are yellow-tipped, passing through pale to dark

green at the stalk. The calyxes of the lower flower (2) and of the buds (2, 6) are moss-green, darker on the side in shadow. The buds themselves are shaded in red and rust.

As mentioned, the pistils are pen-drawn in black when the paint is quite dry.

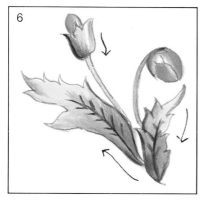

Leaves

The flowers so far examined have been painted, for the most part, in tones of one colour; however, to suggest the shading of leaves satisfactorily, another method is used.

First, have ready on the palette all the pigments required: for example, yellow and buff, chestnut-brown and the various shades of green—pale, jade and moss. Keep them fluid by stirring with the palette-knife and adding oil if necessary. Load the brush and blend the tints as needed, as you would for water-colour: you might take up some yellow, perhaps, with a touch of green and chestnut-brown. This avoids abrupt contrasts which would jar since the shading should imitate the naturally graduated colouring of foliage.

The treatment of various leaves

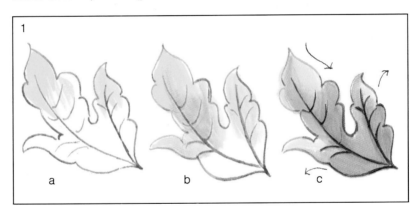

1
a   b   c

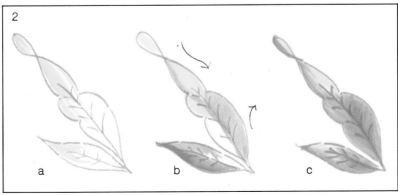

2
a   b   c

is broken down into stages as shown here. The outline of the first leaf is drawn in pen and lightly brushed with yellow at the tip (1a). This is then shaded into pale, and then dark, green (1b, 1c). Fig 2 has a twisted tip and another, lesser, leaf at its base. Here, too, we see the outline, with painting begun in yellow (2a); the green shading (2b); and the leaf completed (2c).

Fig 3 shows two leaves, one half-twisted over. Its underside is painted with curving strokes, outwards from the veining to the edge.

The serrated leaves (4) are of more complex shape and their colours purely autumnal. The tips and indented edges are painted in yellow, over which the chestnut-brown shading is brushed outwards from the central vein. For all these leaves use a No 3 or 4 brush.

Stems

The pen outline of stems must be executed with particular care, for the drawing is of paramount importance.

In the first stage of Fig 1 a stem has been filled in with light, even, vertical strokes, in yellow-buff; in the second stage, small horizontal strokes are added in brown, from top to bottom and left to right, when the buff paint is dry.

The slender green stems (2a, 2c) are shaded first with pale and then with darker green. The noded stem (2b, 2d) is shaded vertically down its length, and horizontally at the nodes.

Below, right, is a group of inter-laced stems (4), each one painted a different green after the outline has been drawn in pen. The oriental-type stem (3) is shaded with a series of lines and dots running lengthwise to give an impression of thickness. Colours here are buff and brown.

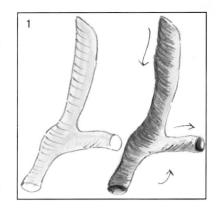

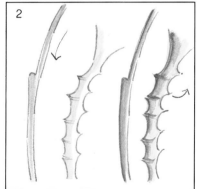

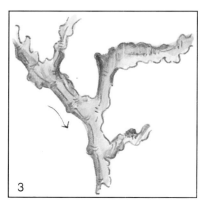

BOUQUETS AND SPRAYS

Porcelain and majolica

Having studied the fundamental brush-strokes and a selection of practical exercises and designs, you will have learned to hold a brush correctly and be able to paint several sorts of flowers, including roses, together with their stems and foliage. In short, you should have gained sufficient skill, experience and suppleness of hand to enjoy painting on china.

We have also looked at a few simple compositions—the bouquets or small sprays on page 56, for instance. Now it is time to go into more detail about such motifs.

The word bouquet, meaning a posy or prettily assembled bunch of flowers, comes from the French. The china-painter's bouquet is a decorative motif, often the most important part of a design, which tends to echo the slightly stylised charm of eighteenth-century traditional designs. The possible varieties of shape and the overall structure of the bouquet are seemingly endless, for there is infinite scope for imaginative and individual arrangements. There are two golden rules

to abide by: stick to nature rather than inventing leaves or flowers and in the matter of stylisation follow the accepted models, at least until you have developed a genuine creative style of your own.

The elements of any composition, the leaves and flowers, large and small, must blend into a balanced and pleasing whole, which should be in harmony with the shape of the piece being decorated, while much of the final effect is due to the choice and placing of colours.

First, then, plan the overall design. Next, draw it in detail before transferring it to the ceramic surface, and consider the size, composition, colour and the separate elements of the design in relation to the piece chosen. A delicate design, perhaps reminiscent of Sèvres, is excellent on porcelain, but majolica suggests something less sophisticated, though not therefore less attractive.

Different techniques are used for these two main types of ceramic. In the pen-drawing of a design on porcelain, leaves and stems are chestnut-brown and flowers are outlined in the colours they will be painted; on majolica the whole bouquet, when pricked-on, receives a black pen outline.

To make this line stand out as it should, reduce the amount of fat oil in the pigment. For the actual painting on majolica, however, the paint needs slightly more oil than for porcelain.

1

Small bouquets

The examples shown in Figs 1, 2, 3 and 4 are all outlined in pen first. They are then painted with a No 2 or 3 brush in one or more of the following colours: rose-purple, pink, shades of yellow and red, violet, pale and moss-green, and light and dark blue.

For monochrome the pen-drawing is in a darker tone of the chosen colour, while for poly-chrome it may be in black or

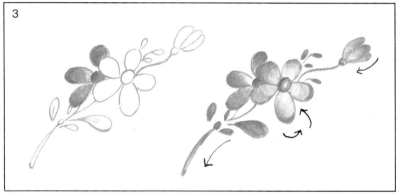

chestnut-brown, always of darker tone than the brushed-on colour. (Adjust the amount of fat oil accordingly.)

For the mixing of the more fluid pigment required for the brush-painting see pages 36–7.

Sèvres-style bouquets

For these typical designs the very light outline, after pricking-on, is in chestnut-brown.

   With a No 4 brush, paint a central flower first—the rose, for instance, in the illustration opposite—then the flowers round it. Lastly paint the buds, the centres of the flowers, and the leaves and stalks, with a No 2 brush. Butterflies or tiny leaves will contribute harmony and balance, completing the design.

2

A polychrome bouquet

For this you need rose-purple, pink, yellow, blue, violet and grass-green. Brushes are Nos 2 and 3.

Having drawn the design in pen, let it dry before you begin painting. Start with the large rose (1), using the No 3 brush and shading with a horizontal spiral stroke. Work from the middle of the flower out to the petal-tips, which should be very pale. Repeat for the second rose. The petals of the violet and marguerites are darkest at the tips and lighter towards the base; the blue-bells are painted outwards from the calyx. Shade the stems in buff and chestnut-brown.

If there is sufficient room on the ceramic, and you wish to make this graceful design a little more elaborate, you could add further elements (3, 4).

2

3

4

1

More bouquets

The bouquets shown in Fig 1 and on pages 82–3 are in polychrome while Figs 2 and 3 are in monochrome. A glance at Figs 1 and 3 will reveal the difference this makes to the same design.

The method for the multi-coloured bouquets has been described already. Use brushes Nos 2 and 3.

For the monochrome designs the procedure is the same. Draw

2

them directly onto the surface in pencil, then in pen go over the outline of the flowers in blue, intensified by a touch of black to ensure that the outline stands out in the finished painting. Paint the flowers first, beginning with the rose and shading them in the usual way, using a No 3 or 4 brush. Leaves, however, are first brushed over in blue, beginning at the tips; they then receive a second brushing, shaded horizontally outwards from the central vein. Monochrome could easily look flat and insipid, and it is this second brushing, which may also be applied to the flowers, that provides the necessary chiaroscuro effect. If well executed, one-tone designs unfailingly give an impression of delicacy and elegance.

83

ORIENTAL-STYLE FLOWERS

Camellia

Oriental flowers are pen-drawn before being painted in the same way as other designs. They may be outlined in cobalt-blue, with leaves and stems in black or brown; or the whole may be in black. The latter is indeed preferable when the background is to be dabbed-on (see pages 142–3), for against such a grounding a design will stand out best with a black outline.

Use a No 3 brush for colouring, and the strokes you have learned already. For the bud (1), shown in three stages, begin with the front petal and paint in upwards, almost spiral, curves (1a). Use horizontal strokes for the petal opening to the left (1b, 1c).

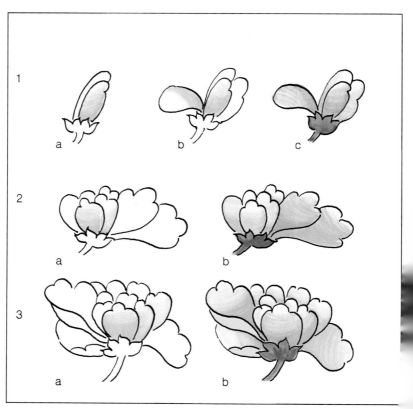

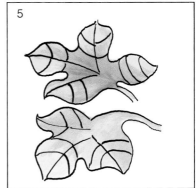

In the second bud (2a, 2b) and for the open flower (3a, 3b), a curved stroke is taken from left to right, with the colour shading off to nothing as it reaches the petal-tips, to achieve a translucent effect. The undersides of the two turned-back petals (3b) can be yellow, as illustrated, a darker tone of the colour in which you paint the flowers—here, blue— or in white relief (see pages 136–7).

Together, these three motifs will make a charming composition (6). Directions for painting the leaves and stem are given on pages 70–2. Some of the details are enlarged in Figs 4 and 5.

Other oriental flowers

The examples shown here also conform to the oriental tradition of flower-design in ceramic decoration.

The marguerites (1) have a preliminary pen outline drawn in black and are painted, with a No 2 brush, in lemon-yellow. Start from the tip of the petal with the usual almost spiral movement, lightening the colour as you proceed. As always, rotate the piece as you paint, so that each petal can be shaped downwards from the tip.

The leaves, too, are painted from the tip, each with a single stroke in chrome- and grass-green.

This motif lends itself to enlargement (see Fig 2 for detail), but you must relate the size of the design to the dimensions of the piece with the utmost care. A lot depends on your 'eye', which can be developed by observing good examples; those in Part Three of

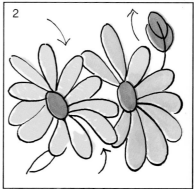

this book will repay close study.

The spray of peach-blossom (3) is also characteristic of oriental patterns. Pen-draw the outline in chestnut-brown and paint each petal from the outer edge with a No 2 brush, shading from dark to very pale pink at the flower's centre, which is yellow. A leaf is painted with a single brush-stroke.

Pen-drawing of the highly orna-mental monochrome design (4) is in deep blue; the flower is painted in cornflower-blue, working up-wards from the centre, with a No 2 brush.

Paint the leaves with light strokes of the same cornflower-blue. When dry, add the shading, which should be taken outwards from the main rib.

Peony

The peony is a classic motif of Eastern ceramic painting. The two versions illustrated—one in red and blue (1), the other pink (2)—are large enough to show the brushwork clearly. This is crucial to the overall effect. On examination, you will see that the impression of roundness in each petal is produced by a convex, edge-to-edge stroke.

The outline is terracotta for the flowers, dark blue for the leaves. Paint the petals, one by one, with a No 5 brush, starting from the base and lightening the colour gradually as you approach the tip (1).

The leaves are cobalt, or another fairly light blue, painted in feathery strokes with a No 3 brush.

The pink peony (2) is another, perhaps more realistic, representation of this flower. The outline of the flower is rose-purple, and

of the leaves and veining, black. Colour the petals pink, with the same convex, edge-to-edge stroke, using a No 5 brush. The flower-centre, half revealed, may be green or yellow. To give the petals maximum emphasis, draw a second outline in pen, in rose-purple or darker pink, almost superimposed on the original line.

The chrome- or yellow-green leaves have further touches of yellow or pale green. Finally, the stem is painted buff and brown.

This is a design for pieces of moderate size.

2

Chrysanthemum

This is another classic motif of oriental decoration; the lance-like, tapering petals, which create myriad shapes, inspire airy patterns full of movement. The vertical design illustrated (2) would suit one of those tall vases which could make a handsome base for an electric lamp. For the adaptation of this design for decoration of such a vase the drawings of the flowers (1, 3) may be enlarged by

means of a pantograph to twice their size, or more, if necessary.

The pen outline will be in violet, rose-purple or chestnut-brown, depending on whether the flower is to be violet, pink or yellow; for the leaves and stem a dark brown outline is best. Once this has been drawn the design is then coloured using a No 3 or 4 brush for the flowers and leaves, and a No 3 for the stems. Shading of the petals may be varied with inward or outward strokes.

The effect of volume is increased if, when the petals have been painted once and are dry, you go over them again for half their length, starting at the base. For the first shading of the stems in buff, take the stroke along the whole length, then add touches of brown.

The technique for painting the leaves is described on pages 70–1.

Oriental-style bouquet

This charming design (see pages 92–3) should be pricked-on, then pen-drawn in black. Paint the peonies pink, the other flowers in different colours and the leaves in various unmodulated shades of green. Brush-strokes for the flowers are those given in the previous pages. For the small leaves and blossoms use brushes Nos 2 and 3; a No 4 or 5 for the larger ones.

Waterlily

Water-plants, especially the tropical waterlilies, appear frequently in the designs on oriental ceramics. Illustrated here are a vertical waterlily pattern (1) and another with a single large flower (4). Figs 2 and 3 show how to paint the central flower of the vertical pattern.

Trace and prick-on the design; pen-draw the flowers in rose-purple, the leaves and stems in black or dark green.

Petals are painted in dark pink. With a No 3 or 4 brush, work towards each petal-tip from the inner part of the flower. The luminous effect comes, as already explained, from the shading-off to a very pale colour, or no colour at all, at the tips. One or two petals are turned over showing some of the underside, which should be painted yellow (2, 3).

Stems and leaves are painted in different shades of green. The biggest leaf in the second design (4) is painted in sea-green, with long, light strokes downwards from the tip; grass-green is used to emphasise the veining. The undersides of leaves, where visible, are in chrome-green.

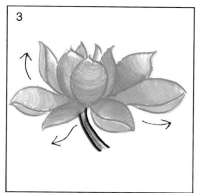

THE ANIMAL KINGDOM

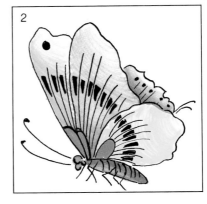

The painting of the butterfly in Fig 1 (seen from above with out-stretched wings) is illustrated in three stages. Shade the wings outwards from the body with a No 3 brush. When the colour is dry, add the black spots with a pen.

The insects in Fig 3 are each shown in two stages. Paint the wing-cases in very light, short strokes with a No 2 brush.

A No 3 is required for the stylised insects in Fig 4; these are also a good choice for

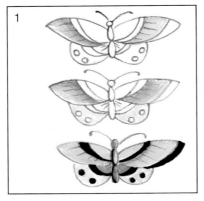

Butterflies and small insects

After flowers, animals are the next most important decorative motif in china painting. The animal kingdom provides an enormous range of subjects including butterflies, insects, birds, fish and shellfish. We begin with designs featuring butterflies and insects; they may either be drawn and pricked-on, or pencilled directly onto the ceramic. The pen outline is black or brown.

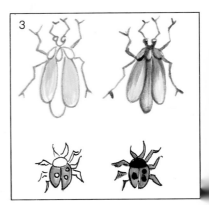

monochrome.

The butterflies in Figs 2 and 6 exhibit the so-called 'Chinese' stylisation of the raised wings. After the pen outline, paint the wings outwards from the body with a No 3 or 4 brush, in the curvilinear stroke previously described. (Fig 5 shows the first stage of Fig 6.) The 'eyes' partly visible at the base of the wings are painted with light strokes. The black pattern-markings on the wings themselves are added last

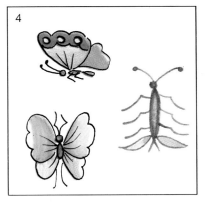

of all, with a pen.

For the examples in Fig 7 use the same technique and a No 2 brush.

Butterflies and insects like these are, for the most part, extra flourishes complementing floral designs: they provide a bright, pretty counterpoint, as in the bouquet on page 76. But they possess an independent decorative value if carefully placed and elegantly painted. They may also be gilded (see page 149).

Birds

Birds have always been a favourite subject of ceramic-painters, as of painters in general. They are especially prevalent in oriental designs and, in common with the rest of the animal world, they are depicted with a certain degree of stylisation. The obvious irregularities arising from this artistic convention are nevertheless accepted, with their distinctive air for tradition's sake.

oil than usual; not too much, though, for fear of damage in the firing.

Illustrated here are three stages in the colouring of a bird (1, 2, 3) painted with a No 3 brush: short yellow strokes for the breast and head (1); the addition of red, avoiding any superimposition on the yellow, which would cause it to vanish during firing (2); and finally the blue. The three birds in Fig 4 are represented in natural settings.

Designs with birds or other creatures are not reserved for pieces of any particular kind. Their use is solely a matter of individual taste, but they should be painted with great attention to the pen line, which should be black or brown and very clean and clear. When it is dry, brush the colours on in light, short strokes that allow the drawing to be seen.

For this light brushwork, mix the pigment with a little more fat

4

Animals in natural settings

Animal motifs obviously offer wide scope for invention and creative ideas; inspiration may be found in the inherited tradition of ceramic art or in works by animal-painters—those of the Baroque period spring to mind; or from direct observation.

A balance must be struck between realistic representation and the stylisation of the creatures depicted; the illustrations given here may be useful as patterns to copy for practice, or as suggestions to develop. The roe-deer on the hillside, for instance, might ornament a box or a pintray (1); a pair of storks in flight, one with open beak, forms a striking pattern against blue, abstract clouds (2). The terrapins with characteristic markings on their shells (3) make a challenging subject to execute. The herons (4) face each other in a heraldic design with decorative symmetry.

1

Pheasants

There exists a separate corner in china decoration for what is known as 'game'. These themes are often taken from those of art in general which has, indeed, always treated the hunter's prey as a subject for specialists; as a genre these paintings tend to be commissioned by patrons, and then to become items of interest for collectors and antiquarians.

While we may legitimately look to tradition for a starting-point, we must, here as elsewhere, exercise our powers of innovation. Adapt what you borrow to a personal expression; add fresh detail. You will thus create individual patterns as distinct from mere transfers which, acceptable as they may be, belong to the realm of mass-production.

The king among game-birds is the pheasant. Our two designs, of

1

the cock bird on the ground (2) and the hen perched on a stone (1), may be painted in true-to-life colours.

Proceed in the usual way with the preliminary drawing on paper, the pricking-on, pen-drawing and brush-painting. The pen outline is brown, mixed with a little black for extra definition. Begin by painting the head, some of which is done in light strokes of buff, and let the brush-strokes flow together to produce a mingling of tints as you proceed with blue, brown or other colours. Use a No 3 or 4 brush and pay attention to light and shade, leaving highlights of a very pale colour.

Do not expect to succeed immediately, for pheasants are no easy undertaking; there is always the scraper (page 22) to turn to which permits repainting if you happen to go wrong but practice will ensure success.

2

Fish and shellfish

In the painting of marine life—fish, shellfish, seaweeds—some stylisation is also the rule. Here are shown two stages in the painting of an exotic fish (1, 2), crabs (4, 5), and an acquatic plant (3). The red pen-drawing—even the plant is outlined in red—gives them all a splendid liveliness.

Choose bright colours in the red-yellow range, using grey for the shadowing, and brushes Nos 3 and 4. Any of these motifs would look well on vases, storage-jars or wall-plates in a seaside house, and may be used for more demanding projects, such as the dinner-service on pages 200–1.

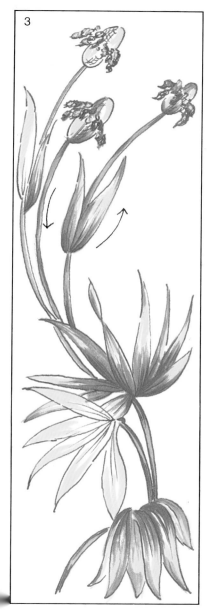

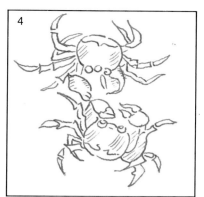

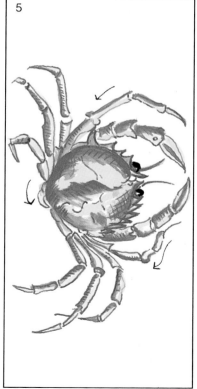

FRUIT AND VEGETABLES

Aubergines, peppers, peas, radishes

Decorations of fruit and vegetables are often termed 'rustic': cottage-style painting on majolica, for the country kitchen and table. The method is the familiar one of preliminary drawing on tracing-paper, followed by prick-ing-on the design and outlining it in black pen.

Paint with a No 4 or 5 brush. A good many colours are needed and, as always when this is the case, have every one mixed and ready on your palette or tile.

For the aubergines (1) put the highlights in with yellow, then shade with violet to suggest the rounded shape. The peppers (2) could be painted in several colours or in monochrome using red or yellow.

Green is the obvious choice for pea-pods (3) and leaves. Remember to paint the highlights first with dashes of yellow, and use different greens for different parts of the plant.

Radishes (4) have highlights left in white; the darker parts and shadows are painted red. Shade the leaves of all these vegetables in colours varying from yellow to pale and moss-green.

By adopting these designs you should soon be able to paint other vegetables from nature, in the same 'rustic' style. A set of wall-plates in majolica, each decorated with a different vegetable, could add a finishing touch to a country-style kitchen.

Peaches

Fruit is a source of inspiration which provides equally charming decorative motifs, but in fact presents a more severe test of skill and exactitude in technique than other subjects. Proficiency will be gained only by experience and is needed especially for the shading process since fruit is represented half in light and half in shadow in order to give it a three-dimensional roundness.

Shown here are the four steps in painting a peach, starting with the brown pen-drawing (1a).

Note that the hanging leaf actually makes the fruit simpler to paint. The first colouring is a light wash of yellow (1b) with a No 4 brush, after which green and red are added (1c, 1d).

A gradual darkening of tint, together with the direction of the brush strokes, suggests the spherical shape and the substance of the fruit.

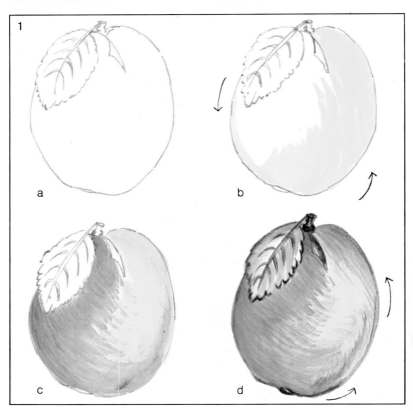

1

a

b

c

d

Strawberries, blackberries, apples

The apple, shown here painted in two stages, and the strawberry and blackberry (shown in three) are all outlined in brown. Work with brushes Nos 2 and 3.

For the strawberry, mix a suitable shade of red, and make the first, light application leaving one side of the fruit paler than the other (2a); a second coat, with strokes closely following the contour (2b), gives volume. The speckles are marked last, in darker red, and the leaves and stalk are painted in tones of green (2c).

A blackberry (2d) consists of clustered globular drupels, each of which is painted with a darker and a lighter half; the latter may even be left white. This fruit, too, dictates its own colouring, which should be a dark red-brown.

Paint an apple (2g, 2h) as you would a peach, using yellow-green.

2

a

b

c

d

e

f

g

h

109

1

Designs with fruit

The strawberries in Figs 2 and 3 form a rectangular design, pen-drawn in brown. The painting is less straightforward than it might appear and is done with a No 3 brush, beginning with the fruit in strawberry-red. Arrows indicate the direction of the strokes. Stems and leaves are green and the flower-pistils are added last, with a pen.

The fruit-and-flower basket with its ornamental ribbon (1) is an intricate subject for cake-plates, dishes with pierced rims and similar elaborate pieces of china; do not attempt it until you are competent and well acquainted with painting the fruit in earlier examples. Having pricked the pattern onto the surface, pen-draw the basket, leaves and fruit in brown, the grapes in dark blue and the ribbon in rose-purple. It will take many hours of patient work.

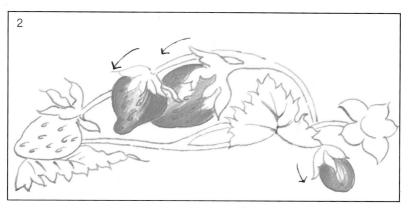

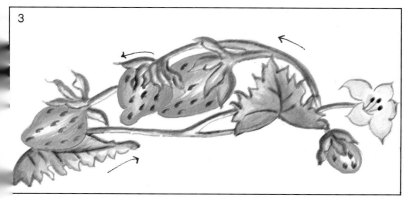

LANDSCAPE

Trees

Another familiar theme of ceramic decoration is that of landscape, with trees much in evidence. Some typical shapes are pictured here (1, 2). Foreground trees are always of darker and deeper tones than those in the distance.

This principle holds good for every landscape element: lighter colour suggests receding distance, which is, after all, how things appear in nature.

For painting tree-trunks the technique is the same as for flower-stems (see page 72): pen-drawing, in black or brown, then a light brushing in buff, with a sense of roundness imparted by additional shading down one side when the paint is dry. Brushes are Nos 3 and 4.

1

Landscapes in colour

Landscape is not, as generally supposed, the most difficult subject for ceramic painting. It is certainly less difficult than repeated geometric patterns, for instance, where minor wobbles of the pen or brush quickly righted in a landscape, can ruin the entire design. In landscape painting the main problem is that of perspective—how to give the impression of depth.

This illusion of depth is obtained by line and colour. The foreshortening of architectural elements is shown in Fig 7 on page 117, and it is usually safe to say that the farther off an object is supposed to be, the smaller it is drawn. When colouring, as already mentioned, an impression of distance is conveyed by progressive lightening of tone.

Three consecutive stages of a landscape may be studied in the accompanying illustrations (Figs

1 opposite, 2 below and 4 over-
leaf). The design, pricked-on after
tracing, is pen-drawn (1). The pen
outline, which for a polychrome
landscape like this example should
be black or brown, is then 'hatched'; that is, certain areas are
shadowed with short, fine strokes
of the pen which lend solidity to
the objects and depth to the composition as a whole (2). Next,
paint with a No 3 or 4 brush, in
delicate strokes that will not obscure the drawing (4). Allow

blank spaces for highlights.

Brush over the hatched parts
again, when dry, to throw them
into relief: you will see how the
light and shade of the rocks arises
from the overpainting of the hatching in black or brown, and the
same procedure, in appropriate
colours, is carried out throughout the picture. Thus, the light
and shade of a green meadow may
be indicated by darker green over
the hatching. Overall colour is, in
a way, secondary to the drawing

2

3

in ceramic landscapes. The basic framework of the scene is drawn in; colour is there to enhance it.

The motifs in Figs 3, 5, 6 and 7 might be incorporated into large designs or used as small independent compositions.

Trees always dominate landscape designs, and for their marvellous variety of forms we may consult art as well as nature. As regards the painting, the technique for the trunks has already been discussed. Tree-tops (for

4

which see also the illustrations on pages 112–13), having been pricked-on and pen-drawn, should be carefully hatched in pen before colouring. The hatching of trees, incidentally, calls for a lot of practice. It has to be fresh, flowing and spontaneous, with nothing rigid or monotonous about it, and put in with a sure and inventive touch; otherwise the result will be stiff and artificial.

Paint trees more or less as you do landscape: a first wash of colour, with some blank spaces left for highlights, then a second brushing over the hatched shadow. Brushes to use are Nos 3 and 4.

Monochrome landscape

Ceramic painting, remember, is decoration, a way of adding beauty and value to objects we handle every day, and its relation to reality is therefore of a special kind. Each decorative element, as we saw in flower, fruit and animal motifs, is not derived only from nature; by virtue of the stylisation that governs its portrayal it is also part of an accepted artistic tradition.

This is true of landscape as well. The two-phase landscape shown here (1, 2) is 'realistic' insofar as its constituent elements —lake, trees, the little cottage and figures on the bank—make up a recognisable scene. They recall real things and people and can be interpreted as such. Yet it is at the same time wholly unrealistic to depict a scene such as this entirely in shades of blue. The choice of monochrome, as well as being highly traditional, is a mat-

1

ter of artistic taste and purpose. For instance a monochrome pattern such as this might, indeed, be recommended for a modern dinner-service; its sober elegance will suit contemporary surroundings.

The real/unreal quality, moreover, is also evident in the construction. The line of the riverbank and trees describes a circle. The crowded lower right-hand corner is balanced by the space at the top in which two birds in the air seem to close the circle; all this contributes to the 'unrealistic' charm.

As before, start by pricking-on the design. Draw it in pen, the hatching in dark blue, with a little additional black for emphasis. Paint with a No 3 brush and lay on the blue in short, light strokes that leave the drawing clearly visible.

2

Dutch landscape

Thanks to the vicissitudes of history, Holland has wielded an influence on European culture quite out of proportion to her size; or, rather, to the size of the Netherlands, of which she is, strictly speaking, a region. In its brief heyday in the seventeenth century the Dutch Republic not only produced a magnificent school of painting, but developed other forms of decorative art which then spread across the western world in the wake of her commercial interests.

There exists a Dutch style of ceramic painting which includes landscapes whose natural or man-made features—waterways and windmills—are typically those of Holland. Three or four examples include windmills and one (3) shows a watermill. These patterns can be modified by the addition or duplication of certain details, and adapted to pieces in porcelain or majolica of all shapes. But,

4

whatever you do, you must judge carefully the area to be decorated as a proportion of the space available: the size of the piece must accord with that of the design. If one or the other is too big the final effect will be either weak or coarse. Proportion is vital in decoration of any kind and a study of the descriptions and photographs on pages 157–240 may, as previously suggested, help to train your eye.

Whether you prefer colour or monochrome for the landscapes, proceed as before with transfer, pricking-on and pen-drawing. Insert the hatching carefully and do not obscure the outline when you paint. Use soft colours, and brushes Nos 3 and 4.

English-style landscape

When England took the lead from Holland in trade and manufacture, her commercial dominance was reflected everywhere as English taste replaced Dutch style.

England's countryside tended to predominate as a subject for china painting, and with it came an echo of the 'sentimental' attitude to nature, pre-Romantic to begin with, whole-heartedly Romantic later on. Today, we are accustomed to dip into the universal artistic heritage, taking eclecticism for granted, and can welcome it among the repertoire of styles.

Of the two designs illustrated, one is autumnal, set on the banks of a rural stream (1) and the other depicts a little manor-house, with an old fortified keep behind it (2). Both provide guidelines for origi-

1

2

nal composition if, when familiar with the examples in this book, you wish to try your hand at other landscapes.

In Fig 2 everything is grouped round the central keep, which dominates the design. In contrast, in Fig 1 the interest is lateral; its side groupings (that on the left being the more important), resemble the wings of a stage and lead the eye, along a diagonal line of vision, to the background. These examples, each with its ad-missible internal logic, represent two of the many ways of con-structing a picture.

The drawing itself is the hard-est part of these designs, as they include many architectural ele-ments whose foreshortening has to be in correct perspective. In the rural scene (1) there is also a succession of receding planes; note how the trees grow smaller in the distance. Draw the hatch-ing with great care and paint with a No 4 brush.

Landscape with figures

The people present in the landscapes illustrated so far have been small and subordinate to the main theme, whereas in the two designs shown here, both glimpses of peasant life, they dominate the surroundings. The style of these pastoral scenes is highly idealised—inspired by the high-flown Arcadian yearnings of the eighteenth-century beau monde fashionable society.

First a farm-girl with flowing garments, a basket of fruit on her head and another in her hand, is depicted in a becoming attitude framed by plants and trees. This would be a delightful motif for a set of plates and is accordingly illustrated in monochrome, for which brushes Nos 3 and 4 are used; or it might be painted in several colours as a single motif. The drawing must be executed with a touch which is at once soft and firm.

1

The country tableau with three figures (2), of more open composition, is also in the style of the eighteenth century. Interest is focused on two figures—the man seated beneath the tree to the left, and the woman opposite. Pictorial links between these points are the strongly emphasised tree on the left bending towards the centre, and the haymaker standing behind the woman, who leans from right to left.

This is, evidently, a compli-cated and fairly difficult design to draw. The brown pen line should not be too heavy, in order not to detract from the graceful rococo style, though the tree, the green bank, the building and parts of the drapery will need plenty of hatching, also with pen.

Paint with a No 4 brush, leaving very pale or white high-lights. This scene, unlike the preceding one, has been executed in full colour, with lively and charming effect.

2

A landscape with floral border

This landscape, enclosed in a garland, differs from others examined in that the shading of trees and hedges is accentuated not by hatching but by the scrolls and curves of the pen outline itself. There is no intermediate step between drawing the outline and the painting.

Blue has been chosen here, though the scheme could be multicoloured or in monochrome of rose-purple or grass-green. For monochrome, the pen-work is carried out in the intended colour, or else in black or brown. Paint the smaller details with a No 3 brush, and larger areas of the setting with a No 4. For the trees use a downward stroke, darkest at the edges.

If you prefer, lightly brush-paint the whole design and let it dry before putting in the shadows with tiny, hyphen-like touches. The garland, incomplete in the illustration, is of course a full circle. Like the landscape, it could be treated as an independent motif, but the two together are a splendid combination with which to adorn a plain piece of china.

126

Oriental landscape and figures

A milestone in the history of china painting was the introduction to Europe, when England and Holland were great commercial powers, of porcelain from China. Porcelain was something absolutely new and not until 1708, at Meissen, did anyone succeed in copying it. But from Meissen the secret spread to other centres, and with it the characteristic motifs of the Orient. So it was that ceramic painting came to include, as did so many of the decorative arts, the sophistications of chinoiserie, of which we give some examples: bamboo shoots against a landscape background (1), a fantastical Chinese landscape with a pagoda (2), and a pair of Chinese ladies (3, page 130).

The landscapes are pen-drawn, with a fairly definite outline, in black or brown. The latter is used in the bamboo design, where there is some hatching on rock and mountains; the shadows, too, are brown, put in with a No 3 brush. Note the white gaps in the stalks—a simple stylised interpretation of the nodes on a bamboo stem.

The chinoiserie with the pagoda —or perhaps it is a little Chinese pavilion—is similarly pen-drawn in brown, then brush-painted in various colours (2). The technique, as can be seen from examination of the picture, is the same as explained in the preceding pages.

4

a

b

c

Two characteristic motifs of oriental decoration appear in Fig 3, together with a couple of stylish ladies. The detailed painting of their heads is illustrated in three stages in Fig 4.

They are drawn on tracing-paper, transferred to the ceramic surface and pen-drawn in the usual way. The pen outline, and any hatching, should be done in two colours: red, suggesting smoothness, for the faces (4a), and black for eyes, hair, the hat worn by the lady on the right, and for their flowing robes. Paint with a No 3 brush, beginning with the heads (4b, 4c).

The figures are 'modelled' by shading along the folds of the drapery, but beware of overdoing this. Chinese ladies possess a certain calligraphic elegance, which should not be blurred.

These oriental designs are suitable for ceramics of almost any shape, especially vases, cache-pots and wall-plates.

GEOMETRIC DECORATION

Greek key pattern and other borders for majolica

Geometric, or repetitive, patterns are nearly as old as the craft of pottery itself. What is an almost inexhaustible repertoire of motifs may be increased by using one's

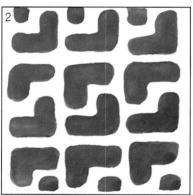

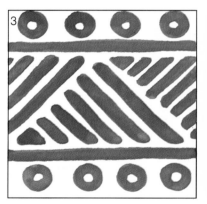

imagination or by borrowing from the many different styles of ceramic painting and other decorative arts. You might try your hand with the dozen or so patterns shown here.

They are 'rustic' patterns, suitable for use on wall-plates, umbrella-stands, bowls and items of that sort in majolica. The repetitive elements of the design are generally arranged round the edges of the piece—along the rim of a plate, for instance—and the

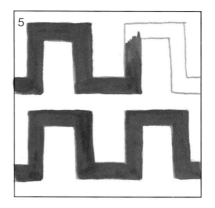

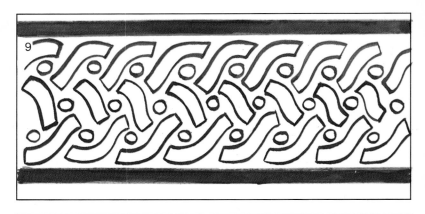

design may be completed by a symmetrical motif (1, 7) radiating out from the centre. The aptitudes required for this type of decoration are not quite those learned hitherto. Here, any irregularity will be at once painfully apparent, and the main concern is to keep the pattern regular and exact while maintaining that intangible quality by which hand-painted decoration is distinguishable from mechanical reproduction.

The complete design is first pencilled onto the piece, then painted with a No 3 brush. Work from left to right applying a sufficient amount of paint in small strokes, which are then blended with long, well distributed strokes, for a close, uniform finish.

The lines enclosing a geometrical border are of matching colour and painted with a No 7 brush.

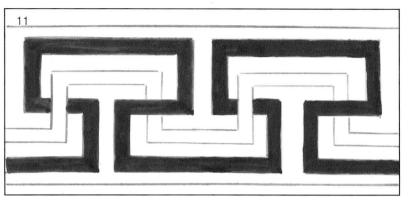

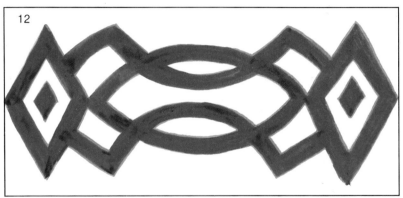

SPECIAL TECHNIQUES AND FINISHING TOUCHES

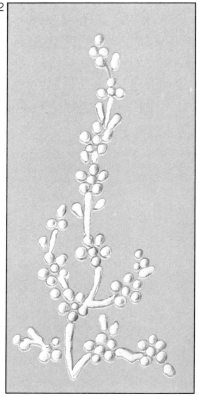

White relief

This is a highly specialised technique by which the decoration is created on the ceramic, almost like sculpture, from the thickness of white paint. It demands especial care and some advance precautions but the results are very rewarding.

First and foremost, have everything scrupulously clean, for the slightest accidental trace of another colour will show up disastrously in the firing. The glass palette for mixing the paint, the brush—a No 1 or 2—and even the oils you use should be kept solely for the purpose of white

relief painting too.

The preparation of the paint is most important: it has to be dense and well mixed, without too much fat oil or turpentine, and is applied in little, close-set dots in very thin layers; this is to avoid the white relief cracking or, worse still, breaking off in the kiln. Indeed, the greatest care is imperative with both paint and painting. White relief, moreover, will not take a second firing.

A detail from Fig 2 is enlarged

3

4

in Fig 1 : a twig of small leaves and cinquefoil flowers in solid white relief. Draw a pencil outline as a guide, then lay on the white paint in the thinnest possible layers with a No 2 brush.

Details from Fig 3 are enlarged in Figs 4 and 5. Having pricked-on the design, outline the centres of the marguerites, stems, leaves and leaf-veins in black with a pen. Paint the leaves with a No 3 brush in flat strokes of chrome and grass-green alternately.

5

On-glaze gold

On-glaze, or superimposed, gold decoration is mainly used on porcelain. It is also known as the 'triple-firing' technique, since a third firing is needed, in addition to the initial firing of the pot and the second which fixes the colours.

When the design has been painted blue and red and fired, the gold is laid, as shown, over the blue. (It appears dull and black as you apply it and will not look bright until it has been fired in the kiln.)

Prick-on the pattern and pen-draw the flowers, as in Fig 1, in red or terracotta, the leaves in blue. The highly stylised flowers are painted red with a No 4 or 5 brush, the undersides of the petals being left white. Paint the leaves in small, close strokes with a No 3 brush. As the paint should

be quite runny, mix it with a few drops of lavender oil and only a little fat oil.

The gilding is applied after firing (2). Fill in the blank parts of the petals with short strokes of a No 2 brush and 'pull' the gold as much as you can to cover the surface without crusting. Next, rotating the work towards you, outline the leaves, and gild their veins, with a pen; if the gold clogs at all, dilute it with solvent (see page 45). The piece is then fired again.

The refiring and the cost of gold make this one of the less economical types of decoration.

2

Brushed-on background

The solid brushed-on background is a technique which is more lengthy than exacting, and is another of our artistic debts to the East.

First, the design is painted. For that shown in Fig 1, prick-on the pattern and pen-draw the large blossoms—stylised peonies—in rose-purple, the leaves and smaller flowers in black. Paint the peonies in pink with a No 3 or 4 brush, then the other flowers, red, yellow, blue or violet as you wish; the leaves are painted alternately in chrome- and grass-green, and are each made with a single flat stroke.

When this work is dry you may start the grounding (2). Fill all the spaces between the design with small, close strokes of a No 2 or 3 brush, with paint which has been mixed with a few drops of lavender oil and a very little fat oil.

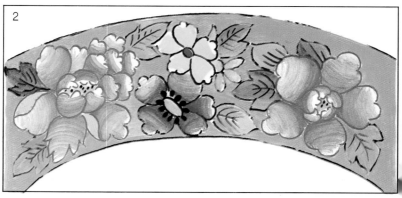

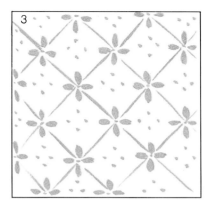

Gilded detail

These three motifs (3, 4, 5) may be used as gilded decoration for any ceramic, though they certainly look best on porcelain. As the gold is not placed over another colour there is no need for the third firing referred to on page 138. Paint with a No 2 brush.

A preliminary outline, if used, should be pen-drawn in black, but you can apply the gilding straight onto the surface.

Dabbed-on background

Brush-painting a coloured grounding onto the ceramic surface—which is, of course, white before decoration—can be somewhat laborious. For a large piece there is the speedier alternative of dabbing-on (see pages 42–3).

Fig 1 shows a bouquet with a dabbed-on ground. The first thing is to position this central design, which is then drawn in pencil or pricked-on from a trac-

ing. Go over it with a pen, and paint it.

When dry it should be protected with a layer of preserving-varnish before you proceed.

Prepare pigment for the background as described on pages 42–3, testing its consistency with a few experimental strokes on the surface of the piece. (Brush No 5 or 7.) If these blend satisfactorily when dabbed, you may safely

continue.

Paint with a well loaded brush, in downward, vertical strokes. Be sure to leave no gaps, however small, and work rapidly, since the actual dabbing can be done only when the whole area is uniformly covered.

Now dab the background lightly and regularly, with a slight overlap. The piece should dry for at least twenty-four hours before firing, and must have another firing if, as in the example, a gilded wreath (2) is brush-painted over the grounding.

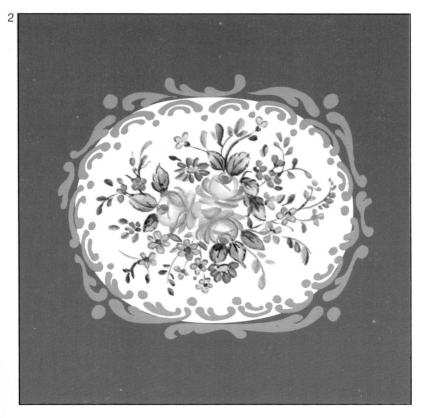

Gold background

The gold ground is of Chinese origin and gives an effect of extreme richness. There is nothing difficult about it, nor does it require an extra firing, as does the on-glaze gilding described on pages 138–9, but it takes time. There is a larger area than usual to be covered —not just the design on a piece, but its entire background—and you must be very accurate, above all when filling in round the design. If you are not fully confident it would be wise to work in two stages, painting and firing the design first, and then repeating the process with the gold.

The three patterns illustrated (1, 2, 3) may be repeated or elaborated to suit various pieces.

The technique differs little from that of other patterns. The design is traced, pricked-on and pen-drawn, the stylised, peony-like flowers being outlined in rose-purple and all other flowers, the stems, leaves and the butterfly (1) in black.

Next begin the painting, using short strokes with a No 2 or 3 brush: pink for the peonies and whatever tints you prefer for the other flowers, bearing in mind that they will be seen against a gilded ground. Leaves are in a single umodulated colour— chrome-, grass- or jade-green. The small abstract curlicues in Figs 2 and 3 may be in emerald-green.

When these colours are dry

apply the gilding with a No 2 brush, in very small, accurate strokes, taking care to fill in gaps between flowers and leaves.

The motifs on these pages may also be used with a brushed-on background (see page 140). The method, and the points to watch, are similar, though the choice of grounding colour is yours. Bear in mind the colours you have already used: a background should act as a good foil, harmonising with the colours of a design.

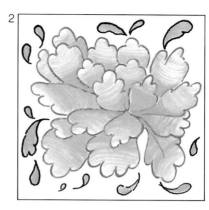

2

3

Gilded ornamental motifs

Ornamental patterning in gold brings a charming hint of luxury to ceramic decoration, not least when supplementing flowers or landscape on a piece of porcelain.

This kind of ornamentation has been mentioned on page 141. Here it is explained further, with a reminder that the effect can be seen properly only after firing, for the paint looks black as it is applied to the porcelain.

Patterns are outlined in black with a pen, and the gold laid on with a No 2 brush. For the small leaf design, paint first the right, then the left, side of each leaf in a single stroke taken from the tip, and leave a white gap in the middle; this prevents the impression of heaviness. Strokes are short (see pages 45–6), with the No 2 brush kept exclusively for gold. 'Pull' the pigment towards you as with colours and rotate the piece as you work, so that you

paint at the right angle.

The motif in Fig 2 may be extended to form a frame for patterns with a dabbed-on ground, such as that on page 143. These designs framed by a border are known as medallions.

On boxes, bonbon dishes and similar pieces the more complicated pattern in Fig 4—a scrolled motif between bands of further decoration—may be repeated horizontally or vertically. It must be executed with the greatest pre-

4

fit a particular piece.

It is worth stating yet again that, despite the degree of precision required for borders composed of repeated motifs, you should strive to maintain the intrinsic, unmechanical freshness of hand-painted work.

3

cision, however, for imperfections would be fatally apparent.

The geometric pattern illustrated in two stages (3) might be used in a single or double line, as a border on the lid of a small box, perhaps round a figurative scene. Leave adequate space between it and the edge of the lid. It looks equally effective in monochrome, for instance in pink or jade-green.

The elegant and graceful motif right (5) could stand alone or be repeated and may be reduced to

5

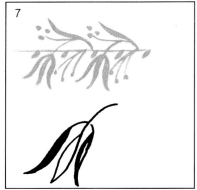

Small decorative motifs in gold

Here is a selection of gilded motifs which, unlike those on the preceding pages, may be used over a dabbed-on grounding. Gold would show up marvellously, for instance, against a ground of blue or green.

Dabbing-on is by now a familiar technique, and whether or not you employ preserving-varnish (see pages 42–3) depends on the

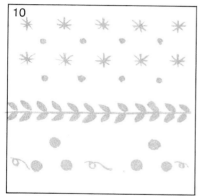

added, with or without little stars, as embellishment or in order to balance more extensive designs, while the lesser butterflies and insects on pages 96–7 could also be used as individual motifs in lighter and simpler designs.

size of the piece. Choose motifs for gilding from the accompanying illustrations, or from other sources, and pencil them onto the grounding after the first firing. Apply the gold in short but dense strokes with a No 2 brush. The designs in Fig 11 are recommended for plates and little boxes, those in Fig 10 for coffee-cups, on which they may form an overall design, or else each motif may be arranged as a frieze.

The butterflies (12) might be

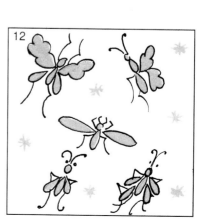

Monograms and crests

The cipher of intertwined initials may complete a decoration or appear as a motif in its own right on cups, bowls and sweet-dishes, on brooches or pendants. A piece of china, especially if in everyday use, will be valued the more for a monogram.

Figs 1 and 3 illustrate a few of the multitude of monogram styles. The letters of the alphabet

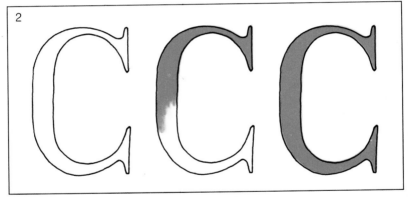

may be combined in innumerable ways—two by two, or three by three for more than one Christian name, or a double-barrelled surname; combined, too, in innumerable scripts, ancient and modern.

The main question is not how to do the painting, but how to entwine the letters and so create the pattern. Study your sketches again and again and try different lay-outs until you are satisfied.

You can then add flourishes, arabesques and flowers and leaves, as the fancy takes you.

Give some careful thought to the colour: gold, perhaps, or a colour from these illustrations—something in tune with the rest of your scheme, at all events. Use the same colour, or black, for the pen-drawing (2), and fill in the outline with brushes Nos 3 and 4.

The crest has a traditional and definite role in ceramic painting.

4

A coat of arms may be single, or double (4) in order to indicate an alliance or a marriage; with a coronet (4); or with a full crest with lambrequins (5). Its function is to convey information about the family from which the object's owner comes.

Apart from this, crests can be purely decorative and the invention of imaginary ones for wall-plates or vases is a fascinating pursuit. With the aid of a book on heraldry or an armorial you may evolve designs from the highly picturesque and often magnificent coats of arms of ancient noble houses.

The drawing, pricking-on and pen outline are quite straightforward. Draw the outline in brown or black and shade the crest in the correct heraldic colours in order to make it stand out. Brushes for the examples shown are Nos 3 and 4.

5

Final touches

Handles, rims, feet and spouts are painted, in gold or in colour, when the decoration is otherwise complete. They are the last, indispensable touches, enriching the design and endowing the work as a whole with grace and charm.

For the solid gilding on the handle of the classically styled cup (1a) the brush should be well loaded and the full strokes evenly distributed. Blue or green might be chosen for the elegant and delicate handle-motif in Fig 1b, while gilding emphasises the attractively twisted handle (1c) on a 'Victorian' cup. A band of dog's-tooth ornament is painted inside the rim.

The jugs in neo-classical and Sèvres style, Figs 2 and 5 respectively, feature elaborate handles; in both, the gilding, as is usual with such pieces, enhances the beautifully wrought shape.

The foot of a majolica bowl or

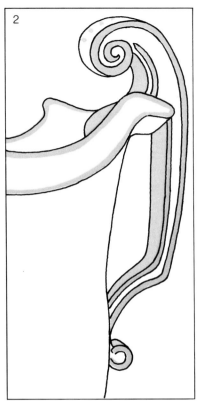

tureen in eighteenth-century style (3) may be painted, with brushes Nos 2 and 3, in gold or in a colour; green, blue or rose-purple would be suitable.

Fig 4 shows another attractive handle, on a porcelain cake-plate with a gilded rim.

Lastly, two types of handle for teapot or tureen lids are shown in Figs 6 and 7, the former with gilded fluting and gilding at the base. The second, in the rustic style so right for majolica, is

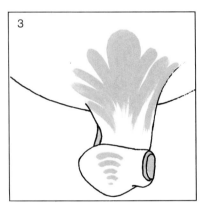

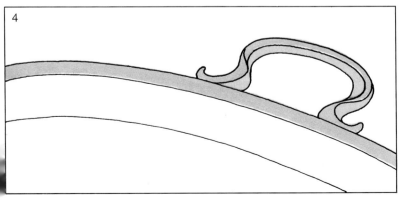

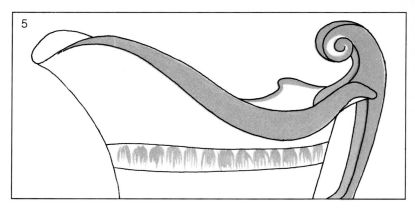

modelled in the shape of flowers and fruit; these are painted in natural colours, the red and green being dabbed over a preliminary wash of yellow.

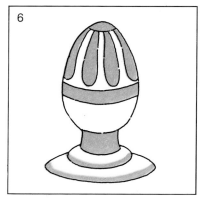

Examples

WALL-PLATE IN THE STYLE OF EARLY MILAN POTTERY

This majolica plate with moulded rim has rustic decoration in the eighteenth-century style associated with the factories at Milan.

The small detached flower motifs making up the garland may be arranged more, or less, symmetrically according to your taste.

The outline is illustrated above. First enlarge it with a pantograph (see page 30) to the size suitable for your plate, then prick it on and draw a dark pen outline in black (pages 31–3). Choose bright colours for the flowers—pink, violet, rose-purple, yellow, sky-blue and dark blue—and paint with soft, semicircular strokes from the centre of the flower towards the petal-tips. The shading should be strongly marked, and a few drops of fat oil will keep the pigment suitably tacky. For the leaves, on the other hand, use a flat unbroken stroke with a loaded brush. Suggested colours are jade-, moss- or dark green.

159

MAJOLICA JUG WITH MONOCHROME DESIGN

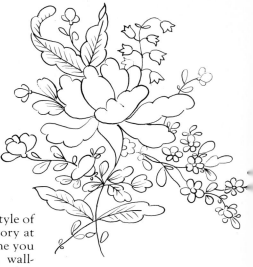

This rustic pattern, in the style of the eighteenth-century factory at Lodi in northern Italy, is one you could use for fruit-plates, wall-plates, bowls, jars and other pieces in majolica.

With a pantograph (see page 30) enlarge it to the requisite size,

and prick-on the design. The pen line, in black, should be very distinct. The jug, illustrated opposite with the pattern in grass-green, could be painted in shades of pink, with a rose-purple pen-drawing—Lodi designs are particularly suitable for monochrome —or even in several vivid, cheerful colours, provided they are carefully chosen and matched. Leaves, in chrome- or grass-green, are painted in single unmodulated strokes taken upward to the tips. Finally, the white background may be scattered with ladybirds, small insects and curlicues (see pages 96–7). There are similarities between this design and those on pages 86–7.

SOUP-CUP WITH LID, DISH AND MONOGRAMMED PLATE WITH FLORAL BORDER

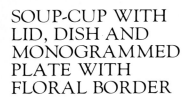

Before transferring the garland pattern shown here mark its central line lightly in pencil on each piece; this precaution will help you to position it properly.

Pen-draw in black, except for the cinquefoil flowers, which are outlined and painted in violet. (If pink is preferred, the pen-drawing is rose-purple.) The smaller leaves are coloured pale green, the larger ones moss-green tipped with yellow. Buds, red and lavender-blue, need no initial pen line.

DISH, PINTRAY AND ASHTRAY WITH SMALL FLOWER DESIGNS

The enclosing ornamental line on the dish shown top in the illustration is drawn in terracotta with a pen. The ears of corn are rose-purple and gold; the overarching spray of flowers and foliage which frames them is pen-outlined in black and the blossoms painted red and black with inward-curving strokes working towards the centre. The leaves, painted half chrome- and half dark green, are shaded off to the tips.

The round pintray is decorated with a 'Lodi' bouquet in green (see left, below, for design). This should be enlarged to an appropriate size, pricked-on, and the leaves and flowers outlined in black. The leaves, coloured grass-green, are shaded off at the edges;

the main flower is darkest at its centre and the petals, painted from the base, are paler towards the tips.

The third piece, an ashtray, has a bunch of anemones in various colours and tiny leaves. Draw the outline in black, and when painting shade the petals outwards from the middle of the flowers. A narrow gold border completes the design.

VASE WITH BUTTERFLIES AND FLOWERING BRANCHES

The illustration below gives details of part of the design on the front of the vase opposite. The motifs making up the rest of the design, which covers the whole vase, are given on pages 168–9.

For an object as large as this the pattern is best treated in sections to be pricked-on one at a time (see pages 31–3), with due regard for the spacing of each section in order to achieve an overall balance. Draw the pen outline in black, then paint the flowers lilac-blue, the centres in darker blue and, occasionally, red to make a lively contrast which will enhance the composition. The small leaves, grouped in twos and threes, are

each painted with one flat stroke of yellow-brown. The butterflies fluttering through the design are pen-drawn in black. The basic colour for their wings must be kept fluid, and is therefore mixed with a little fat oil. It is applied in short strokes, and should gradually be shaded off to a very pale tone as you move away from the body. The additional 'eyes' in red bring out the iridescent texture.

A band of deeper tone marks the outer edge of the wings; the body may be buff or yellow.

As well as being suitable for vases this pattern could be adapted for the base of a lamp or a rectangular centre-piece for the table, either using the whole design or just some of the motifs. These may be enlarged or reduced as necessary by means of the pantograph (see page 30).

MAJOLICA TRAY WITH 'STRASBOURG' FLOWERS

The bunches of flowers decorating this square tray are in the style of the *fleurs de Strasbourg* produced there during the second half of the eighteenth century.

The pen outline of the blossoms and leaves is black, except for that of the central flower of the large spray and the roses in the lesser corner-sprays. For these use rose-purple, and break the pen line into tiny hooked strokes in order to give lightness to the petals. Roses are palest at the centre, darkest towards the petal-tips. Paint the leaves grass-green, with the veining penned in black.

A double border of grass-green gives the tray an elegant finish.

171

COFFEE-CUPS WITH DECORATIVE BANDS

Four identically shaped coffee-cups are illustrated opposite, each with a different design.

Given the cylindrical shape of the cup and the concave surface of the saucer, here too it is helpful to split the patterns into sections and prick them on one at a time. The vine-leaves and tendrils (1) on the cup and saucer shown at the bottom of the illustration opposite are in red, gold and turquoise. A plainer and more linear design (2) is carried out in gold (see pages 146–7, 148). The effectiveness of the design (3) on the cup at the top of the page depends on the colours chosen; we suggest red, green-blue and gold. Since the scheme is rich enough as it is, the saucer is left plain save for lines, one blue, one gold, round the rim. The remaining cup and matching saucer (left, in the photograph) has fanciful leaves and flowers in gold (4). The handles of the three cups in the foreground are gilded (see page 49), though you might choose a less difficult treatment, or prefer the plain white handle shown on the cup at the top.

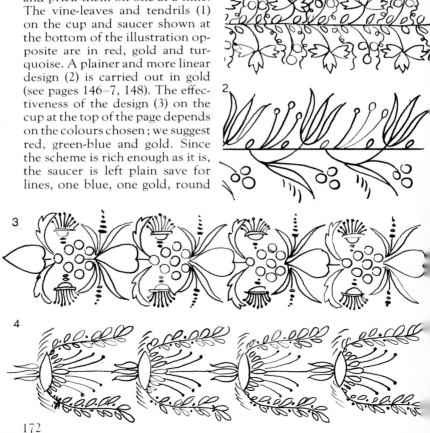

PORCELAIN VASE WITH ORIENTAL DESIGN

The oriental-style design shown opposite on a cylindrical porcelain vase consists of a simple flower-spray with a bird.

It is pricked-on (see page 31) in sections, and the flowers are pen-drawn in what is to be their final colour (here, rose-purple). As you paint, lighten the colour from the outer edges of the petals towards the flower-centre, which is completed with yellow stamens and black pistils (see pages 68–9). The leaves are shaded in tones of chrome, moss-green and yellow. The brown shadings of the twig are applied over a first coat of buff (see page 72) and the bird's plumage is shaded in yellow, blue and brown.

For the finishing detail of the painted rim, gold would obviously add to the beauty and richness of the vase.

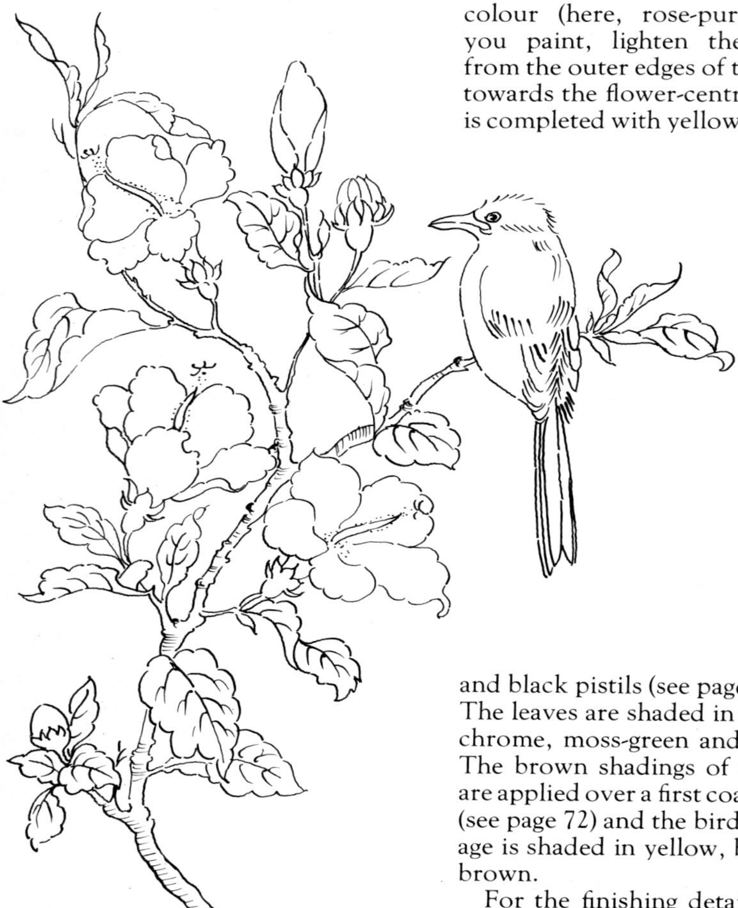

MAJOLICA BOX WITH CHINESE DECORATION

Ceramic boxes of all sizes are among the most rewarding of objects to paint, and a majolica piece such as that illustrated may be bought from any good stockist.

The oriental landscape motif on the lid is a slightly reduced version of the outline shown below, left. Draw it to the dimensions you need with a pantograph (see page 30), then prick it on and give it a brown pen outline, which should be neither too faint nor too heavy. The robes of the little Chinese figure are brightly coloured in pink and yellow; paint them lightly, then pick out the folds with tiny strokes in a darker tone. The rocks are brown, with the chiaroscuro brought out by descending brush-strokes; for this, mix the paint with turpentine or a few drops of fat oil to keep it soft. The grey-blue colour of the water, too, should be applied with very soft strokes. The alternating pale and moss-green of the grasses is painted with single small strokes made from top to bottom without lifting the brush.

It is traditional to decorate the interior as well as the lid of the box and the design (below, right), though no more than a sprig of buds and leaves, lends distinction to the piece.

PEN-POT WITH BOUQUET DESIGN: RIM AND BASE IN GOLD

The motif on the porcelain desk-pot opposite is reproduced, on the same scale, above.

Prick-on the bouquet and pen-draw it lightly in brown. (A little extra fat oil in the pigment will give the correct consistency for this.) The hanging pink flower to the left is fringed with drop-like pistils; after a first light brushing, go over the middle part of this flower again, when dry, to give the effect of shadow. Leaves are chrome-green, in varied paler and darker tones. As a finishing touch which further harmonises the composition, fill any gaps with feathery grey strokes.

The other side of the piece, not seen in the photograph, bears a monogram in gold, set between two delicate motifs of twigs,

flowerets and foliage also in gold (see below).

The gilded handle and rims complete the design. Gilding, as previously noted, requires a second firing.

CAKE-PLATE WITH ROSE AND TULIP DECORATION

This square baroque-style plate carries a bouquet design featuring a rose and tulip, surrounded by small insect motifs.

The pen-drawing, in brown, is very light with the pigment being mixed to a soft consistency with a little fat oil (see pages 36–7). Pen-draw the rose in rose-purple and paint it the palest pink; only the petal-tips, from which the brush-stroke is taken downwards to the middle of the flower, are slightly darker. The tulip is in tones of violet, edged with yellow (see pages 66–7).

The raised parts of the moulded border are accentuated by gilding.

PLATE WITH TURKISH-STYLE DECORATION

The composite design and the colour scheme of this plate recall Turkish ceramics made at Iznik in the sixteenth century.

Prick-on the pattern and go over it with a clear pen line in black. The three dimensional effect of the tall central feather is suggested by painting its outer, or nearer, side a darker colour than the inner side; make long downward strokes with a fanned-out brush. The rib of the feather is then painted red.

Round the rim of the plate is a border of flowers and leaves in alternating blue and green, within a double line of blue.

SMALL BOXES WITH DECORATED LIDS

first of the two suggested designs, in the foreground of the photograph opposite, is a bouquet with a central rose painted, to match its pen outline, in red or rose-purple. The marguerites are a delicate turquoise and the other flowers yellow (see page 64). The extra strokes of grey are very pale. Gild the wreath of leaves round the bouquet, then dab-on the grounding (see page 42) in the typical Sèvres turquoise.

The second example has an oriental design of Chinese jugglers. Here the pen outline is black, with red for hands and faces (see pages 130–1). Paint each of the figures in bright distinctive colours; broad strokes, with the brush fanned out, will give light and shade, and thus volume, to the robes. Finish the painting and fire the piece before the hinge is fixed (see pages 50–1).

The boxes in the background of the photograph are similar in shape to those whose lids have been described here.

From the mid-eighteenth century onwards the celebrated French manufacturers of ceramics at Sèvres and Limoges specialised in the production of small decorative objects. Though majolica was also used, most were in porcelain—such things as medallions, pendants and little boxes with or without lids. The painting is that of the miniaturist, subduing his imagination to this more restricted shape, with its requirements of balance, attractive colouring and economy of outline.

Subjects for this kind of piece should be chosen with care. The

TUREEN AND STAND WITH FLORAL MOTIFS

The majolica tureen shown opposite, with its curving handles and pear-shaped knob on the lid, is unmistakably eighteenth-century in style: a delightful piece, with a 'rustic' design reminiscent of those used in the north Italian factory of Lodi. (See below for the motif on the body of the tureen, above for that on the lid.)

Enlarge both patterns to the required dimensions with the pantograph (see page 30), trace and prick them on (see page 31). Make the pigment for the black pen line fairly tacky with a little fat oil. Small flowers, butterflies and insects may be scattered over the remaining surface (see pages 96–7).

Paint the rose in a darkish colour and shade it off from the centre to the much paler petal-tips, which can even be left white. The leaves, in light and dark green, are also painted with upward strokes, towards the tips.

The modelling on the side-handles is picked out with ornamental lines, while the pear and leaves on the lid are first painted, then dabbed-on in yellow, red and light and dark green (see page 156).

WALL-PLATE WITH SHIP DESIGN

This is another Turkish-style design for a wall-plate, to set beside that on pages 182–3.

Prick the pattern on in the usual way and make a clean, definite outline in black. Instead of painting the design next, as for previous examples, now dab the whole plate in pale blue. With a scraper (see page 22) remove this background from the design itself and key to it the colours you select: yellow for the sails, green, red and yellow for the ship's side and some of the decorative detail. The poop-deck is dark green, and the parts seen under water are a lighter tone of green. The sails are first brush-painted with downward strokes, then dabbed over to shade the colour off. An irregular line encloses a border of fanciful motifs and scrolling.

BOX AND PINTRAY WITH GILDED DECORATION ON DABBED-ON GROUND

The lid of the box illustrated shows a bird against a landscape background. The design is pen-drawn very lightly in black and the bird painted in tones of blue —dark, sky-blue or lilac. The trees behind are in various tones of jade- and grass-green, shaded with a few upward strokes of yellow.

Narrow lines of gilding are added round the rim of box and lid, and gold dots are scattered on the body of the box itself.

directly onto the grounding, thus avoiding any smears of lamp-black. Preserving-varnish (page 40) is then brushed over the design; care must be taken to stay within the outline. Once the background has been dabbed-on, the varnish is removed with a scraper.

The design is outlined in gold with a pen. Brush-paint the bodies of the bird and tortoise in gold and after firing, pen-outline wings, claws and shell in black.

On the right of the photograph is an unusually shaped pintray with a red-brown or terracotta dabbed-on ground. The motifs depicting a tortoise and an imaginary bird may be pricked-on, though it is better, if you are sufficiently adept, to draw them

CACHE-POT DECORATED IN BLUE AND RED

Prick-on the pattern and draw a firm terracotta outline. Colour the stem in dark blue, making the pigment quite thick, for the brush should be well loaded. The petals, unmodulated, are in dark yellow and terracotta. The small leaves

This cache-pot is a modern adaptation of the eighteenth-century bowl known in England as a Monteith; wine-glasses were cooled in the U-shaped notches of the rim. The design on it is chosen to emphasise the shape, typical of faience ware of the period.

are also blue, painted with soft strokes towards the stem. The ornamental lines of terracotta on the base, handles and scalloped rim are applied with a No 7 brush, the colour being mixed with a few drops of fat oil to keep it fairly fluid.

192

COFFEE-SERVICE
WITH BIRD MOTIFS

Illustrated opposite are the cream-jug, sugar-bowl and two cups of a coffee-service, each of which is decorated with a single bird perched on a twig.

All the birds need not be the same. As with the cups on pages 172–3, one motif can be repeated throughout, or different but related motifs may be used: here there is a variety of birds.

The black pen outline should be clear but not too heavy. When this is dry, paint the plumage (see page 98) in colour ranges of yellow to brown, and grey to blue, with short downward and inward strokes. Avoid red if possible, for it will fade in time—sooner than ever on something that is going to

be washed up as often as a coffee-cup. Moths, ladybirds and small insects (see pages 96–7) are dotted about the saucers; their bodies are brown and their wings echo the colours of the birds.

In decoration of this sort, which should be fresh and crisp, nothing should distract attention from the motif; rims and handles are therefore left white.

OBLONG DISH WITH INTERLACED DESIGN

Here is an example of a plain, simply shaped object transformed by the right decoration into something anyone would be proud to possess. The sober and distinguished pattern is in the Rouen style, so named after the French factory where it originated.

Like other designs we have seen, this is best divided up. Prick it on in four sections, making sure that they fit together exactly and that the black pen outline is very distinct.

When this stage is dry, paint the continuous scrolls round the sides in dark and pale yellow. The handsomely framed latticed motif in the middle of each side is red. Small leaves and flowers are green and lilac-blue respectively, and the design is much enhanced by the surrounding band of cobalt-blue. Prepare the colour for this background carefully, with a little fat oil and a few drops of lavender oil; the brush has to be well loaded and the paint must spread well in order to achieve the flat, dense covering required. When the first coat is dry, go over it again with long, neat strokes.

PORCELAIN DINNER-SERVICE WITH FISH DESIGN

The main attraction of this decorative scheme is the fact that no two plates are alike and no motif is repeated. The fish and the background patterns vary: a fine opportunity for exercising the imagination which, in addition to the pleasures of design and colouring, makes china painting the expression of personal taste.

On this and the opposite page are some of the motifs from the service illustrated on pages 200–1. After pricking-on (see page 31) they are outlined with pen in red. For the charming little fish below, painted in red and lilac or grey-blue, soft brush-strokes are taken outwards from the middle of the body, while the seaweed is painted red, yellow and grey, so lightly as to be almost transparent. The technique is the same for the fish on the opposite page, the only difference being the addition of yellow and pale grey.

Other sea-creatures and aspects of marine life—the crabs, perhaps, on page 105—might be included.

The twisted knob of the, tureen, with its rococo curls, is entirely red and gold and every piece of the service has a thin gold rim, which should be painted using a banding-wheel.

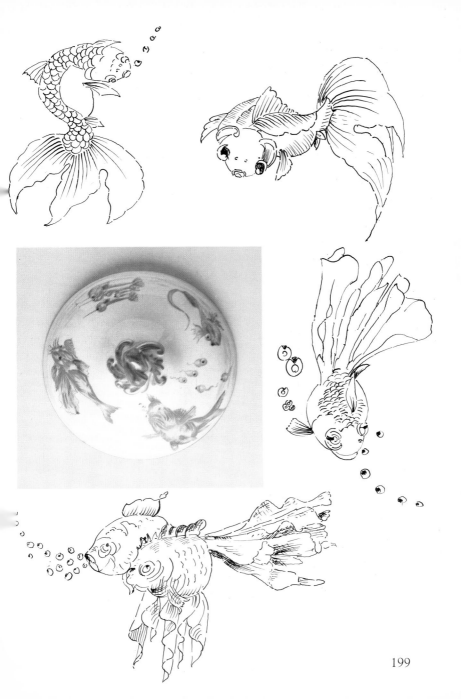

PLATE WITH 'ROUEN' PATTERN

The design of this porcelain plate is based on one of the most characteristic eighteenth-century patterns in the Rouen style. The colours of the reproduction are as near to the originals as possible.

The dominant motif, both in terms of size and variety of col-ours, is the cornucopia on the right, which is balanced by a brilliant bird among flowers and branches on the left. Small insects are scattered at random, and a butterfly at the top completes the composition.

Prick-on the design and draw the outline in black, with a firm, even line. The many colours needed include yellow, red, green, brown and blue, all applied with light, soft strokes.

BOWL WITH FLORAL PATTERN ON GOLD GROUND

The porcelain bowl seen opposite is decorated with an oriental-style frieze on a gold background. Though rich and complex, this demands exactitude and patience rather than exceptional skill.

ciding whether the stroke should be inward or outward (see page 59). The leaves are painted alternately in chrome- and grass-green, with long strokes towards the stem.

When the pattern is finished paint the gold ground with full, short strokes, using brushes Nos 2 and 3. 'Pull' the gold as much as you can, to prevent crusting, and add a few drops of diluent (see

Begin as usual by pricking-on the design, here reproduced on a small scale. Pen-draw the larger flowers in rose-purple and everything else in black. These large flowers are to be painted pink, the others in whatever bright colours you may choose. Work with brushes Nos 3 and 4, in semi-circular strokes. The movement is mostly from the flower-centre to the petal-tips, but study each blossom individually before de-

page 45) should it become too thick. It is best to paint always in the same direction, vertically from top to bottom.

If you are in the least doubtful about tackling this process, fire the piece when the design is finished and paint the background afterwards. Your colours are thus fixed, while any imperfections in the gilding are easily eradicated with the scraper (see page 22).

PORCELAIN JAR
WITH ART
NOUVEAU DESIGN

An art nouveau motif here decorates a porcelain jar of classical shape.

The design is uncomplicated and uncluttered, one side depicting a dragonfly, with stylised clover-leaves and flowers. This motif is pricked-on, and pen-drawn in brown. When colouring the dragonfly's body in yellow and brown, make the left side of each segment darker than the right. The upper wings are pink, the lower violet, painted with long, soft strokes, shaded off from the centre outwards. The clover-leaves and stems are pale green, with brown shading. Ribs, veining and the banded markings on the leaves are in gold, the flowers violet.

An ornamental knot-pattern in pink, green and violet occupies the other side of the jar, and these colours are repeated in the interlaced border running below the rim.

BOX AND PINTRAY WITH DABBED-ON ROSE-PURPLE GROUND AND GOLD EDGING

Reproduced above is the bouquet, consisting of two roses with marguerites and other flowers, which decorates the box illustrated opposite. When pricked-on the pattern is pen-drawn in rose-purple; the roses, painted in the same colour, are shaded off from the centre to the tips of the petals (see pages 60–1). The remaining flowers, including the marguerites, may be in various bright colours and should be painted with a loaded brush. The tiny leaves are in alternating chrome-and pale green, the larger in grass-green. A few feathery strokes of grey complete the composition.

Use the same technique, and a similar motif, for the pintray.

Remember to define in pencil the space for the bouquet on both pieces before dabbing-on the background (see pages 42 and 142–3). The scrolled frame round the bouquet is pricked-on when the piece has been fired (see page 31); outline it first in gold with a pen, then fill in by brush-painting in gold. Next the rims of box, lid and tray are gilded and the second firing follows.

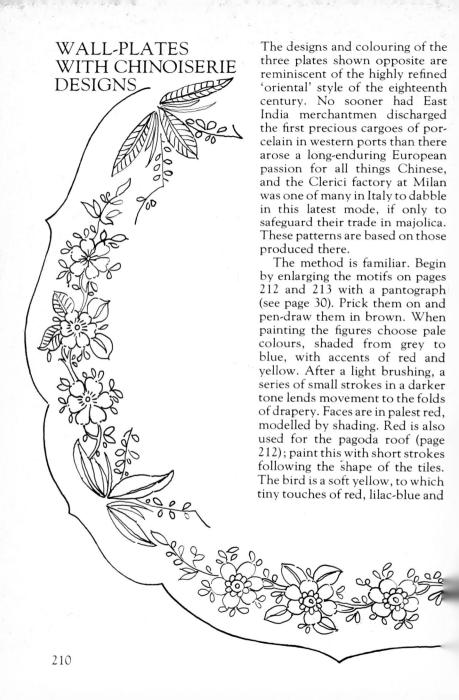

WALL-PLATES
WITH CHINOISERIE
DESIGNS

The designs and colouring of the three plates shown opposite are reminiscent of the highly refined 'oriental' style of the eighteenth century. No sooner had East India merchantmen discharged the first precious cargoes of porcelain in western ports than there arose a long-enduring European passion for all things Chinese, and the Clerici factory at Milan was one of many in Italy to dabble in this latest mode, if only to safeguard their trade in majolica. These patterns are based on those produced there.

The method is familiar. Begin by enlarging the motifs on pages 212 and 213 with a pantograph (see page 30). Prick them on and pen-draw them in brown. When painting the figures choose pale colours, shaded from grey to blue, with accents of red and yellow. After a light brushing, a series of small strokes in a darker tone lends movement to the folds of drapery. Faces are in palest red, modelled by shading. Red is also used for the pagoda roof (page 212); paint this with short strokes following the shape of the tiles. The bird is a soft yellow, to which tiny touches of red, lilac-blue and

violet are added, suggesting the plumage. Butterflies are in bright tints, with curvilinear brush-strokes taken outwards from the yellow bodies. Flowers, with petals painted outwards from the centre, are in various tones of yellow and lilac-blue.

The leaves are painted alternately in chrome- and grass-green, with flat, unbroken strokes from the edges inwards, and the earth, or terrace, where the figures stand is softly brushed green or light grey; little strokes of various shades of green indicate the blades of grass. The border of leaves and flowers illustrated on page 210 is executed the same way and in the same colours as those of the central designs; it may be divided, for the sake of exactitude, and treated one section at a time.

LAMP WITH CHRYSANTHEMUM DESIGN

A lamp is one of the most popular pieces with beginners and a suitable vase may be majolica or, as in this example, porcelain.

The design illustrated covers the entire surface and should be enlarged to at least twice the size shown above; when pricking it on (see page 31) pay great attention to the balance of the overall arrangement. The pen-drawing is in dark blue, with a touch of black added to the pigment if a more definite outline is desired. Flowers, stalks and leaves are painted in the same blue.

These blossoms, though fantastical, recall the chrysanthemums on pages 90–1. Work from the flower-centre in curvilinear strokes, shading off to each petal-tip. Paint the stalks lightly, then shade them with a second brushing on the left-hand side (see page 72). The leaves also receive a first light brushing and are shaded afterwards; paint outwards from the rib of the leaf.

The piece is then fired. A second firing follows when stem, leaves and leaf-veins have been pen-outlined in gold.

214

VASE WITH PAINTED WHITE RELIEF

Much of the ornament on the porcelain vase illustrated is carried out in painted white relief (see page 44).

Bouquets are at the centre of medallions enclosed by raised white lines, surrounded in turn by interlaced sprays of cinquefoil, some in painted white relief, others painted in one colour.

The design is pricked-on and the bouquet cleanly and firmly outlined in pen. Flowers which are to be painted pink are outlined in rose-purple at this stage, and the rest in their intended colours. Leaves, veining and twigs require a much finer, black pen line.

It is important to emphasise the shading on the petals as you paint. For this, mix a slightly more tacky pigment than usual and work with a fanned-out brush in half-moon strokes down towards the centre of the flower.

The leaves, of alternating chrome- and grass-green, are painted with full, unmodulated strokes. Tiny strokes, set very close together like a series of dots, will increase the prominence of the white relief.

A delicate border, pen-outlined in terracotta and brush-painted in gold (see page 45) runs round the rim of the lid and the top and bottom of the vase itself.

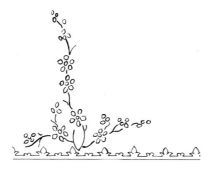

WALL-PLATE WITH MULTICOLOURED DESIGN

The artistic appeal of this plate lies in the complex floral and animal design—a miscellany of creatures as diverse as fish, ducks and mythological birds.

Begin by marking off the border with two concentric pencil lines (see page 19). The pattern is best treated in sections, pricked-on separately (see page 31). Glance occasionally at the illustration on pages 220–1 as you proceed: it may help you to attain the compositional balance and due proportion of patterned to unpatterned surface that makes for a successful effect. The border, too, is dealt with in sections corresponding to the cartouches, or medallions, round the rim.

The whole design is then pen-outlined in black. As this outline should not be too obvious the paint may be mixed with a little more fat oil than usual, to keep it tacky.

The colour scheme effectively contrasts every possible tone of grass-green and blue. The flowers are shaded lightly in dark blue or buff (see page 59). Paint them with curvilinear strokes, from the centre out to the petal-tips, with a gradual lightening of colour to achieve a luminous, fragile look. Since they do not all lie in the same direction, turn the plate and work on each flower from the most convenient angle. The grass-green tops of the flower-heads, above their base of blue or buff flowerets, are built up of minute clusters of dots, penned in black, and the flowers on the left, faintly resembling dandelions, are done in the same way. The body of the bird on the right is green, blue and yellow; paint is applied with small strokes and shadows are emphasised in black with a pen. The fabulous bird at the top is also yellow, green and blue, with the colours slightly shaded off towards the upper parts of body and wings.

The fanciful motifs in the medallions, and the little flowering branches next to them, are brown and green. For intervening segments of the border, formed of stylised leaves and pale brown marguerite-like flowers, brush on the background lightly in grass-green, having mixed the pigment with a few drops of lavender oil until it is soft and runny (see page 41). This grounding is then scattered, not too thickly, with black pen-dots, and the leaves are painted a darker green to make them stand out clearly against the background.

221

CACHE-POT WITH LANDSCAPE DESIGN

Almost any type of decoration would fit the plain shape of this majolica cache-pot, and we have chosen a design in the oriental style.

The scroll motif in the foreground is pen-drawn in rose-purple and painted in the same colour with brushes Nos 3 and 4; work inwards from the edges in vertical strokes. The roses, too, are pen-drawn in rose-purple and shaded off, when painted, to the petal-tips. The pen outline for the rest of the pattern is black.

The branch and the leaves of the roses are painted, with shading, in grass-green, as are the trees. The detached small leaves are also grass-green, but in a paler tone, with alternating light and heavy strokes.

The background landscape is pen-drawn in dark green but painted in a lighter tone; this gives a sense of distance and perspective.

FRUIT-DISH WITH PIERCED RIM

This elegant porcelain dish with pierced edging consists in fact of two separate pieces, foot and bowl.

This is a good point to note a general rule which should always be followed: before you embark

leaves and stems. The flowers are painted red with half-moon strokes taken from the centre and shaded off towards the petal-tips. Deep blue is applied with light, close strokes on stems and leaves to ensure an even distribution of

on any kind of china painting take the object you intend to decorate and wash it thoroughly with soap and water. The present example needs more careful cleaning, particularly of the pierced border.

The design illustrated here adorns the bowl both inside and out and for a shape like this should be pricked-on (see page 31) in sections. The pen outline is terracotta for the flowers and the scroll-like fronds, deep blue for

colour. The decoration then receives its first firing.

Next comes the gilding, stems and leaves being outlined in gold with a pen (see pages 45–6). Narrow gold lines enclose the patterned areas, interior and exterior, and the plain white stem of the dish is accentuated by a plain gold line at the base. Lastly, the rim is gilded with a pen, refired, and the two parts of the piece assembled with glue (see pages 50–1).

224

PLATE AND VASE WITH DABBED-ON GROUND AND DECORATION OF SMALL MOTIFS

The plate with pierced rim and the vase shown opposite exhibit a minimum of decoration—a scattering of small roses on the plate, a small landscape framed in a central medallion on each side of the vase. Their main appeal is in the colour of the yellow dabbed-on background (see page 42).

Prick the designs onto the surface and go over them with a pen in black. Flowers are painted rose-purple, the colour being shaded off towards the ends of the petals. The leaves (including the tiny leaves on the rim which need not be arranged symmetrically) are in alternating light and dark green. The miniature landscapes, in matching positions on the sides of the vase, are painted in lilac-grey with short shaded brush-strokes to create a chiaroscuro effect. (For monochrome landscape see pages 118–19.) The work is then fired to fix the colours.

Before you start to dab-on the grounding (see page 42) cover what you have already painted with preserving-varnish (see page 40). This is removed with a scraper (see page 22) when the dabbed-on colour is dry, and the pieces are then fired for the second time.

227

GOLD-RIMMED PLATES IN RED AND DARK BLUE

These dinner-plates are decorated in what is known as a *Compagnie des Indes* design; that is, in the style of porcelain made in China for export to Europe in the eighteenth century. They are decorated in three stages, and three firings are required.

Begin by marking the central circle and the double lines of the border in dark blue, using a banding-wheel. Fire the plates for the first time.

Next, transfer the pattern to the surface. Prick-on, one by one, the four sections making up the pattern on each plate, and divide the border, too, into separate sections. Pen-draw the entire design in dark blue except for the flowers, which are both outlined and painted in red. Paint the leaves blue with a full loaded brush, and fire again.

The third and last firing follows when the leaves and their veining have been outlined in gold (see pages 138–9).

JUGS WITH DUTCH LANDSCAPE DESIGNS

The classic eighteenth-century shapes of these two porcelain jugs perfectly accommodate the chosen landscape designs, which are pricked-on from tracing-paper and pen-drawn in brown.

The colours should be shaded on with soft light strokes (see pages 114–15, 116) and the pigment well mixed. A few extra drops of fat oil will maintain the tacky consistency that allows good effects of chiaroscuro to be achieved.

A floral garland surrounds the lid and neck of each jug with its small roses drawn and painted in rose-purple, the other flowers in blue; pen-draw the leaves in brown and paint them green. Flower-bud handles on the lids are pink, shaded with rose-purple.

The pretty line of gilding between each landscape and the garland above is brush-painted, as are the narrow lines of gold ornament on the spouts and handles.

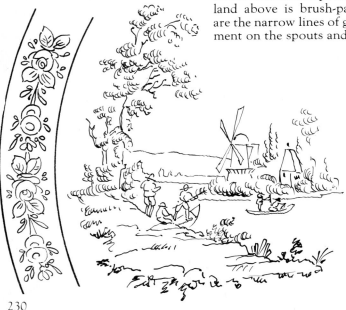

DINNER-SERVICE WITH FLORAL BORDER

Opposite and on the following pages is illustrated a dinner-service in porcelain—plates, sauce-boat and tureen with stand.

Once again, the best way to achieve a balanced arrangement of the pattern (detailed below) is to split it up. When it is pricked-on (see page 31) the flowers are pen-drawn in red, the rest in deep blue. With a No 4 brush paint the flowers a lighter shade of red than that of their outline, shading the

petals in soft strokes with the brush well flattened out and the upward semicircular movement described on page 59. The leaves are deep blue, painted in small close strokes without shading (see pages 138–9); to ensure this uniform impression the pigment should dry almost immediately and be mixed with a few drops of lavender oil and not much fat oil.

The flowers of the central motif on each plate are also outlined in red, and the leaves in deep blue. Paint as for the border and give the first firing.

Next, gild the rims and draw in the other gold outlines with a pen. (Any errors or smudging are soon put right with a clean rag soaked in gold diluent or, better still, in water.)

Handles, not forgetting the knob on the tureen lid, are painted gold, red and deep blue before the second firing.

VASE WITH MULTICOLOURED FLORAL DESIGN ON BLACK GROUND

The complete, and highly complex, flower design for the vase seen opposite is given on pages 92–3 (see right for detail) and is easier to handle if pricked-on in separate sections.

It is pen-drawn in black, except for the peonies, whose outline should be rose-purple. They are brush-painted in pink, while the other flowers are yellow, red, lavender, blue and violet. Shading is obtained with a curvilinear stroke, soft and light, starting from the centre of the flower; leaves, too, are painted in lightly modulated strokes. For the lid, whose pattern is shown below, the procedure is the same.

A black grounding is now brushed onto the parts left white (see page 41), including all the small spaces round and between the flowers and leaves. Use small close brush-strokes and mix the black pigment thoroughly with turpentine, a little oil of lavender and not too much fat oil.

The final, luxurious gilding of rims and base requires, of course, a second firing.

JUG WITH
BOUQUET MOTIF

The decoration on this jug is a spray of varied flowers and leaves, a detail of which is used on the other side of the jug. The nature of the composition is such that it demands accuracy of detail in the drawing and a subtle elegance of colouring.

Divide the design into units, as in the case of similarly intricate

compositions, and prick them on as neatly and accurately as possible, placing the whole with care.

The brown outline should be very lightly traced in pen, so make and keep your pigment fairly tacky to ensure delicate contour and shadow-effects. The colour is applied with soft light strokes with very little modulation, so that it sets off this faint outline; again, therefore, mix the pigment with a few extra drops of fat oil. The flowers—or, rather, buds—are pink; the smaller leaves are grey, the larger ones are alternately pale and turquoise-green. The fluting where the handle joins the body of the jug is lined in grass-green.

SOME DECORATIVE MOTIFS

1 12 13 15 Bird forms from pre-Columbian ceramics; Mexico. **2 5 8 9 10 16** Small animal motifs; modern. **3 4 17 19** Stylised animals from Chinese popular prints. **6 11 18** Animals from terracotta dishes; New Mexico, AD1000–1200. **7** Bird in red and black from a vase; Cyprus, 750BC. **14** Elk; vase-painting from Susa, Iran, 4000BC.

1 6 Oriental ceramic figures. 2 7 9
10 Animals from pre-Columbian
ceramics; Mexico. 3 Chinese
dragon. 4 8 12 Modern stylised
animals. 5 Lion; from
a bowl made in
Rhodes, 580BC.
11 Islamic motif,
fourteenth century.

1

2

3

4

5

6

1 2 3 4 Seashells and seahorse;
drawn from nature. 5 Octopus
from a Cretan amphora,
1500BC. 6 Fish from a
terracotta plate; New Mexico,
AD1000–1200. 7 Fish from
Chinese pattern book. 8 9
1o 12 Stylised trees; modern.
11 13 Landscapes with trees;
European popular prints.

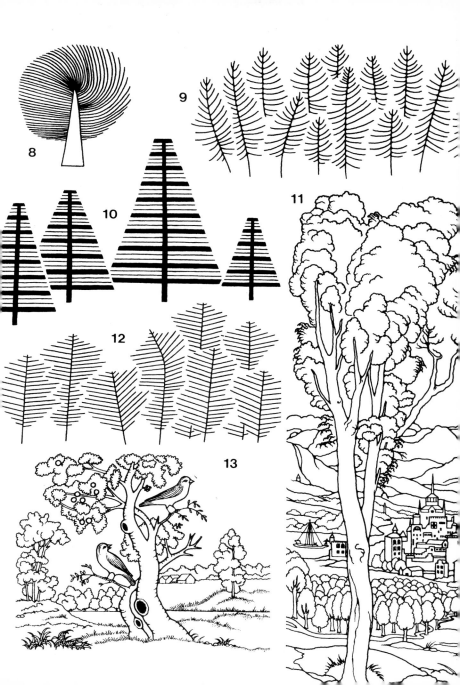

8

9

10

11

12

13

1 4 7 German popular prints nineteenth century. 2 French print eighteenth century. 3 Dancing maenads; Greek ceramic figurines. 5 Details of Florentine print, AD1500. 6 Wood-engravings by Albrecht Dürer. 8 Rococo figurine. 9 Figure from tenth-century ceramic; Iraq. 10 Figure of a musician; Persia late sixteenth century.

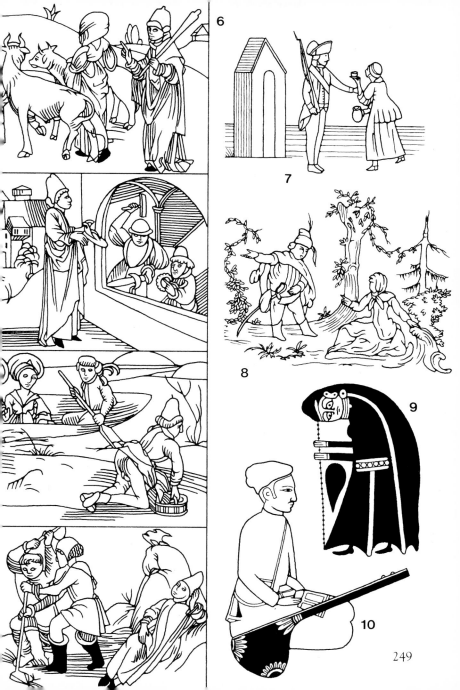

6

7

8

9

10

1 2 3 4 Motifs from African pottery.
5 Byzantine decorative pattern, twelfth century. **6 7** Art nouveau borders.
8 Oriental pattern of flowers and leaves.
9 11 Geometrical border patterns. **10**
12 Decorative patterns; English, early twentieth century.

INDEX